The Gift
of a
Child

JAMIE & KATRINA HOLTOM

the GIFT *of a* CHILD

spiritual lessons from

the life of a child

Northstone

Editor: Michael Schwartzentruber
Cover and interior design: Margaret Kyle
Proofreader: Dianne Greenslade
Cover artwork: "Glowing Lights," Artville
Cover photo of Lucas Holtom by Jamie Holtom

Unless otherwise noted, scripture quotations
are from the New Revised Standard Version of
the Bible, copyright 1989 by the Division of
Christian Education of the National Council
of Churches of Christ in the USA. All rights
reserved. Used by permission.

Scripture taken from the Holy Bible, New
International Version (NIV), copyright 1973,
1978, 1984 by International Bible Society. Used
by permission of Zondervan Publishing House.
All rights reserved.

Northstone Publishing
acknowledges the financial support of the
Government of Canada
through the Book Publishing Industry
Development Program for
its publishing activities.

Northstone Publishing is an imprint of
Wood Lake Books Inc.,
an employee-owned company, and is
committed to caring for the environment and
all creation. Northstone recycles and reuses and
encourages readers to do the same. Resources
are printed on recycled paper and more
environmentally friendly groundwood papers
(newsprint), whenever possible. The trees used
are replaced through donations to the Scoutrees
For Canada Program. A portion of all profit is
donated to charitable organizations.

**National Library of Canada
Cataloguing in Publication Data**

Holtom, Jamie, 1969 –
The gift of a child: spiritual lessons from the life
of a child/ Jamie & Katrina Holtom.
ISBN 1-896836-53-4
1. Meditations. 2. Bereavement – Meditations.
3. Bereavement – Religious aspects –
Christianity.
I. Holtom, Katrina, 1970 –   II. Title.
BV4832.3.H64 2003   242'.4   C2002-911446-2

Published by Northstone Publishing,
an imprint of Wood Lake Books Inc.
Kelowna, British Columbia, Canada
www.joinhands.com

Printing 10 9 8 7 6 5 4 3 2 1

Printed in Canada
at Transcontinental Printing

Contents

Introduction   7
The Gift of a Child   11
The First Night   14
Feeding the Hunger   17
Just Kidding   20
Getting Cleaned Up   23
Routines   26
Smile When You Get Dirty   29
Looking on the Inside   32
Taking that First Step   35
Stuck!   38
A Heart of Compassion   41
Taste and See   44
Sharing Our Toys   47
If You Love Me   50
Fishing for People   52
A Special Day   54
Choosing the Most Important   57
A Wonderful Place   60
Being Together   63
Conky on the Bonky   66
Right Back, Mommy!   69
How Many Times?   72
Mommy Tired?   74
Joy Comes in the Morning   77
Bedtime Prayers   79
No Higher, Pilot!   81

Crazy   84
Crocodile Tears   87
Finally Sleeping   90
Where'd That Come From?   93
Don't Worry   96
Drive?!   99
Excited or Afraid?   101
Getting Sidetracked   104
Happy with Little   107
He Just Knows   110
Hope for the Future   113
Giving Away Roses   116
It's All Good   119
It's Good to See You!   121
A Little Boost   124
Just Throwing Stones   127
Love at Every Sight!   130
Make a Joyful Noise   132
Running the Bases   135
Whose Church Is It?   138
Still Love Me?   141
The Grocery Store Bun   144
The Key to Getting There   146
The Stairs Story   149
Where's Howie?   152
Sweet Memories   155

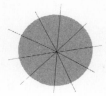

Introduction

It was a warm summer day that the unimaginable happened. Our two-year-old son, Lucas, was killed suddenly and tragically in a tornado that touched down at Pine Lake, Alberta, on July 14. Since that time, we have had a deep desire to honor and remember his life. This book is one of the ways we hope to do that.

In the following pages, we have put together some of the many memories that we have of Lucas. These stories, though not necessarily in chronological order, are all true. For us, these stories are more than just good memories. They contain profound life lessons. How interesting it is that some of the greatest wisdom comes through the eyes and the life of children. Certainly Lucas brought that into our lives.

Our hope is that as you read the following stories you will meet a fun-loving, life-giving, joy-filled, little boy. For at the center of these stories lies a beautiful boy who was precious to many, and whose red hair and blue eyes and infectious smile impacted all who came in contact with him.

Throughout his life, Lucas moved us closer to God simply by the way he lived. It is our belief that these stories and this book will allow

Lucas' life to do the same for others; for as you read these stories, you will meet an ever-present, deeply-loving God, who is full of compassion and tenderness, and who wants the best for all of us. If we open ourselves up to some of these most basic lessons of life, we, too, can discover the simplicity and the joy of a two-year-old.

To our children

We realized, when we put this together, that our daughter Leah was our only child. However, we hoped that our family would grow and that she would someday have siblings to play with and to care for and to share her life with. Happily, that hope came true with the birth of her brother, Cameron.

Leah, we want you to know that we have thanked God for you every single day of your life. We cannot imagine how we would have made it through the first few months after Lucas' death without you. Whether it was your cry in the morning (and throughout many of the nights!), or the need to feed you or change your diaper, you gave us purpose. But more than that, you gave us love in a way that perhaps only you could. As much as you needed us, we needed you. Thank you.

We want you and Cameron, and any other brothers and sisters that might come along, to know that even though we may not have written a book about you, you are just as important. We hope that you will love and cherish your brother whom you were never given a chance to know.

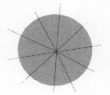

The Gift of a Child

And they shall name him Emmanuel, which means, "God is with us."
MATTHEW 1:23

We first discovered that Katrina was pregnant with Lucas about a month before Christmas, but decided to wait until Christmas to tell my parents. In part, we did this in order to make sure that all was going well with Katrina and baby. However, we also wanted to wait because we had a little prank planned. My parents, particularly my mother, were extremely eager for us to have children. So we thought we'd have some fun of our own when it came time to exchange Christmas gifts.

We went out and bought a soother and wrapped it up for my mom. Within the package we included a note that said, "The rest of this gift isn't quite ready yet; hope you can wait another seven months!" When my mom opened the gift, she was a little shocked. And then she figured out what was going on. She jumped and yelled like a little kid. Santa couldn't have done a better job.

Looking back, I now realize what a wonderful gift Lucas was to us as well. You could wrap up a new set of golf clubs. You could put a bow on a brand new Ford Explorer. You could put two round-the-world plane tickets in an envelope. But they wouldn't even come close to the awesome, precious gift of a child. Ask any parent about their top memories in life and no doubt the birth of their children will be on that list. Children are a gift that we are blessed to receive.

Every Christmas we celebrate the gift of a child. Our Christian tradition says that an angel came and proclaimed to the people of the day some astonishing news. "I am bringing you good news of great joy...to you is born this day in the city of David a Savior, who is the Messiah, the Lord. This will be a sign for you; you will find a child wrapped in bands of cloth and lying in a manger" (Luke 2:10–12).

I don't think for an instant that it was an accident God chose to come in the form of child. Children, our children, are the greatest gift we could ever receive.

- What are you going to do to love your children today?
- What can you do to show the children of this world that they are the very best gift this life has to offer?

A word with God

O God, thank you for coming to this world in the purest image, a child. Open my eyes to the amazing gift of children all around me, to see deeper than the surface and to appreciate their innocence. Today, may my heart be filled with the same love for you as you have for me, and may I show that to everyone in my midst. In the name of that child who came to us so long ago, in the name of Jesus I pray. Amen.

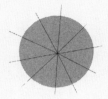

The First Night

Rejoice with those who rejoice and weep with those who weep.
ROMANS 12:15

We were so excited the day we brought Lucas home from the hospital. It was to be our first night at home together as a family. I had made a very simple kindergarten-quality sign welcoming Katrina and Lucas, and had stuck it to the door of our two-bedroom apartment.

As excited as we were, I think we were even more afraid. Now we were on our own. No more nurses to tell us what to do when he cried. No more extra hands to help out during bath time, or experienced hands to wrap him up ever so tightly. This first night was not only exciting, it felt like the moment of truth.

After getting Katrina and Lucas home and settled, I had to go out for a while during the evening. When I returned, I could hear Lucas crying as soon as I entered our building.

As I climbed the stairs, I wondered, what's wrong? Inside, I found our good friend Jocelyn carrying Lucas around the apartment. He was such a little ball in her arms. All you could see was his wide-open mouth as he cried and cried and cried.

We took turns holding him and walking him. Katrina tried to feed him. We changed his diaper. We tried to wrap him up nice and tight. We held him in different positions. We showed him different rooms. All the while he continued to cry. He cried so long that he lost his voice and all that came out was a pathetic, hoarse little squeak. By this point we were *all* ready to cry.

As I think about that night, I realize that one of the things that made that evening a little more bearable was that our friends Jocelyn and Bill were there. In reality, they knew no more about babies and what to do than we did. What made them so valuable was that they were just as ready to cry as we were. They felt the fear we felt. They knew firsthand the frustration we were experiencing. When Lucas actually lost his voice, they felt as much pain as we did. They wanted him to go to sleep and stop crying as much as we did. And later, looking back on that first night, they would laugh just as hard as we would.

In Romans, Paul says, "Rejoice with those who rejoice and weep with those who weep." True friends do that! That was the value of having our friends with us that evening – not that they were able to fix things, but that they fully entered into our lives.

God gives us people who do that, who enter into our lives and love us, who feel our pain and celebrate our victories, who don't just offer us a shoulder to cry on but shed a few tears with us – real people who cheer us on and in doing so encourage us like no one else can.

- Who brings these gifts to your life?
- Who makes those difficult "first nights" more bearable for you? Whoever they are, be thankful for them. I can't imagine life without them.

A word with God

Thank you, God, for friends like these, for those people who make life more fun and more bearable. Thank you for Jesus, the one through whom you have entered humanity and experienced life as we know it, with all its laughter and its tears. In his name I pray. Amen.

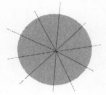

Feeding the Hunger

I am the bread of life. Whoever comes to me will never be hungry.
JOHN 6:35

When kids enjoy something, they *really* enjoy it. It's difficult to divert the attention of a child who is having a great time with something they love. Certainly this "problem" applies to food as much as to anything else.

From a very early age, Lucas developed a deep love for bananas. In fact, there wasn't much that would get him more excited. Whenever he saw a banana, he would repeat "es pease" until his wish had been granted.

If I wanted to eat a banana myself I would have to do so with my back to Lucas so that he couldn't see. Otherwise, I would have to donate at least half my banana to the little redhead.

When you *did* feed him a banana, you couldn't slice it fast enough. As soon as you put one piece on his plate, he'd have it eaten and be waiting for the next. His hand would move continuously from his tray to his mouth, each time picking up a slice of banana and stuffing it in his mouth. Chewing was not a priority. The only thing that mattered was getting as much banana as fast as humanly possible.

Like most of us, Lucas loved to eat. Food is fun and it tastes good and it keeps us going. However, there is a hunger that not even a banana can satisfy – a *spiritual* hunger that is as real as any physical hunger one might have.

God knows that we need to be fed. In the Gospel of John, Jesus says, "For the bread of God is that which comes down from heaven and gives life to the world…I am the bread of life. Whoever comes to me will never be hungry."

When we discover the nourishment that God offers, it is like eating a banana for the first time. Our eyes sparkle with excitement as we discover what it's like to feel connected with a power greater than ourselves, to know that we are loved and cared for by a God who made us.

Some of us may have fed from this source of love and grace for many years. The excitement of a young child reminds us that each time our hunger is satisfied, we are fortunate indeed.

- What are you hungering for today? Can God's love once again fill that place in your heart that needs nourishment?

A word with God

There have been times in my life when, according to the world, everything was perfect; and yet I still felt "something" was missing. My soul hungers for you, dear God, and I pray that your love will continue to feed me. Thank you for this abundance of food for my soul. Help me to continue to reach out for your nourishment. Amen.

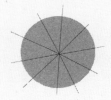

Just Kidding

"For I know the plans I have for you," declares the Lord,
"plans to prosper you and not to harm you,
plans to give you hope and a future."
JEREMIAH 29:11 (NIV)

We were enjoying a wonderful weekend at a beautiful cottage. One morning, my good friend Rob decided to play a little joke on Lucas. As Rob was eating a banana, he held out a piece towards Lucas and inquired invitingly, "Want some?" Then he quickly retracted his arm, said, "Sorry, it's mine!" and popped the last piece into his mouth.

Well, you would have thought the world was about to end, seeing Lucas' reaction. The tears, the devastation, the betrayal! Little did our host know that bananas were Lucas' favorite food *and* that our little one-year-old had a *very* good memory. Later, when Rob tried to give Lucas some banana again, he would have *nothing* to do with it.

For the longest time, Lucas thought of Rob as "the one who took away my banana." And who wants to have a relationship with someone who would do something like that? It took a number of visits and a lot of work before Lucas would "come around" and consider Rob one of his friends.

Some people are suspicious of God in the same way that Lucas was suspicious of Rob. Have you ever heard the phrase, "The Lord giveth and the Lord taketh away"? Is it any wonder that some people would not want to have a relationship with God, if that's really how God acts?

When bad things happen in life, people have a tendency to blame it on God. "How could God have *done* this to me?" is a common cry. Personally, I don't believe that God teases or tests us by playing with our lives to see how we'll handle *this* sickness or *that* death or *these* multiple setbacks.

Jeremiah 29:11, reveals a God with a much different agenda. God says to the people of that time, "For I know the plans I have for you…plans to prosper you and not to harm you."

This doesn't in any way answer every question about human suffering. It doesn't explain why bad things happen to good people. It doesn't imply that "there's a reason for everything." What it *does* offer is a glimpse of a God who seeks the best for our lives. Hopefully, that's a view of a God that more people will want to have a relationship with.

- What do you think God's role is in human suffering? Do you believe that God causes bad things to happen to test us, or do you believe that God desires goodness, wholeness, and healing for you and your loved ones? Is there someone you know who might be encouraged by this latter image of God?

And perhaps the most important question:

- How might this day be different if you saw God as a friend who desires for you to have all the "bananas" you can eat?

A word with God

Loving God, help me to know in my heart that you desire the best for my life, today and always. It is hard to understand some of the things that happen in my life and in the world. Help me to remember that you are about goodness and hope. May this image of you rest in my mind, and allow me to move forward in love and peace. Amen.

Getting Cleaned Up

Create in me a clean heart, O God, and renew a right spirit within me.
PSALM 51:10 (NIV, ADAPTED)

Lucas was taking a nap one day at the babysitters. He always slept well there, and some afternoons he'd sleep for a very long time. On one of these occasions Darlene, Lucas' caregiver, sent her son up to see if Lucas was awake yet.

When Christopher opened the door to Lucas' room, he quickly shut the door again, went to the top of the stairs, and called down to his mom: "Mom, you better come up here. There's a *big* mess!"

Lucas had pooped. This was not the messy part, because of course poop was normal. The messy part was what Lucas had done *after* he'd pooped. He had succeeded in taking his diaper off and experimenting with how this poop might spread. It was all over! It was all over the crib. It was all over his hands. It was all over various parts of his body. It was even in his hair. What a mess!

The funny thing was that Lucas wasn't bothered by this at all. He was as happy as could be! When Darlene walked into the room, there he was, standing up with a big smile on his face.

As happy as he was, Darlene couldn't leave him like that. She took him straight to the bath and cleaned him up. She washed his hands, his bum, his back, his feet, even his hair. I was very glad that Darlene cleaned him up. And though he wasn't too thrilled at first, I'm sure Lucas felt better as well. He certainly smelled better!

Sometimes our lives can get kind of messy. And like Lucas, we can even become content with the mess. That is, until we're reminded of a better way. We may eat poorly until we realize how much better we feel when we eat properly. We may be lazy and inactive, until we rediscover how good exercise makes us feel. We may stop praying or going to church or pursuing God's presence in our lives, until we once again discover the joy of drawing near to our Creator.

It's natural and normal to slide into bad habits that we don't necessarily like. Being negative, yelling at our kids, gossiping, becoming obsessed with money – all these things plus many more can mess us up.

The good news is that God loves us and offers to help clean us up, just as Darlene cared for Lucas and cleaned him up. The only difference is that we need to ask for God's help, like David did when he cried out, "Create in me a clean heart, O God, and renew a right spirit within me."

- Do you have any little messes you want God to help you clean up? God's desire isn't to make us feel bad. God's desire is to make us feel whole, healed, and put-together.

A word with God

Gracious God, today I ask forgiveness for the messes in my life. I admit that I have sometimes let bad habits replace the good habits that honor you. I pray that with your help and love, I can clean up my ways. Thank you for your great love, which makes change possible. Amen.

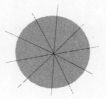

Routines

For everything there is a season, and a time for every matter under heaven:
a time to be born, and a time to die; a time to plant, and a time to pluck up;…
a time to break down, and a time to build up.

ECCLESIASTES 3:1–3

Most of us have a variety of routines that we follow. Perhaps it is a morning routine, or a workday routine, or a routine for meals throughout the week, just to make life easier. For children, it has been well-documented that routine and structure provide a framework for their lives that allow them to feel safe and secure.

As new parents, we were aware of this need for routine, but we were quite amazed when Lucas provided the routine for us! By about three months of age, it was very apparent that our little boy *needed* to go to bed by 7:00 p.m., otherwise he was quite unhappy.

Once we noticed this, we made sure to set up a routine: dinner came around 5:45; then some playtime with Mom or Dad; then watching some TV sports with Dad; then upstairs for a bath, story, and bed; and finally, lights out, good night!

We followed this routine as best we could, wherever we went, and it served us well. As long as we adhered to it, Lucas would go to bed happily, wherever we might be, even if it was a new place. It provided him with a familiar structure that obviously made him feel safe and comfortable, no matter where he was.

We work hard to provide these comforting routines for our kids, but what about for ourselves? Do you ever think about what kinds of routines are best for you? When do you work best? When do you need rest? How do you care for your body? Your mind? Your soul? Have you built into your life those things that make you a better person? Is God part of your routine?

Ecclesiastes 3 says, "For everything there is a season, and a time for every matter under heaven: a time to be born, and a time to die; a time to plant, and a time to pluck up;...a time to break down, and a time to build up." Perhaps it is a meal with the family, prayer, reading, journaling, exercising, or connecting with good friends. There *is* a time for everything. Just as Lucas needed some kind of routine in order to thrive, so it is natural for *us* to work best when we recognize these necessary times in our lives.

- Are you happy with your routine these days? Do you have any changes that you've been thinking about making? Are you caring for yourself as well as you are caring for your children? Don't forget, there's a time for everything.

A word with God

Gracious God, thank you for the different times of life, and for the security of routine. May I find peace this week in performing the routines of each day, thankful for their purpose. I pray that I will continue to make you a regular part of my routine, knowing that your presence in my life makes all the difference. Amen.

Smile When You Get Dirty

A cheerful look brings joy to the heart, and good news gives health to the bones.
PROVERBS 15:30 (NIV)

It has probably happened to most parents at some point. We were out early one morning on the May long weekend, doing what many do at that time of year. We were getting our garden ready.

Our backyard isn't very big and it has a fence, so we felt pretty safe in having Lucas back there with us as we dug up the dirt in the garden. For his part, Lucas was enjoying the time playing with a little hand shovel. He was running it through the dirt and digging little holes as he sat on the grass in his pajamas. This was a new experience!

After planting a few tomato plants, I looked over at Lucas to see how he was doing. As I did, I saw his hand moving up towards his mouth. Nothing too unusual in that except that his hand also happened to be full of dirt! Before we could get to him, in it went. Dirt all over his face and in his mouth. Laughing a little, but concerned, we picked him up and wiped off his face as quickly as we could. It seemed pretty disgusting to us.

But did Lucas care? In the midst of our disgust and concern, he flashed us a smile I'll never forget – a big open-mouthed smile that revealed the pockets of black dirt still in his mouth. It didn't bother him at all. "Don't worry about me, Mom and Dad, I'll be just fine!" his grin seemed to say.

As I look back on that experience, I can't stop seeing that wonderful smile. If only *I* could smile like that when I find myself tasting the "dirt" of life. What a difference it would make to be able to smile even in the midst of difficult moments, especially at the small stuff.

Proverbs 15:30 says, "A cheerful look brings joy to the heart, and good news gives health to the bones." That's the right idea. At some level, we can control our inner response simply by offering a cheerful look. How can we still be angry, if we're smiling?

Over the long haul, we'll be that much healthier if we lighten up through God's gift of laughter, especially at ourselves. A simple smile can take you a long way. Why not try it out today?

- Can you smile when you get the red light on the way to work? Are you able to laugh at yourself when you screw up? Ever try grinning when you miss the three-foot putt? Or when the pot boils over? Or when your spouse leaves the toilet seat up? Can you show your pearly whites when the dirt of life gets on you?

A word with God

Dear God who offers so much joy, I pray that I might try to laugh at those little tastes of dirt I experience this week. Remind me, please, that a cheerful look can go a long way to lightening not only my own heart, but the hearts of those around me. Let the joy abound, and the dirt be minimal! Amen.

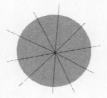

Looking on the Inside

Do not look on his appearance or on the height of his stature,
because I have rejected him;
for the Lord does not see as mortals see; they look on the outward appearance,
but the Lord looks on the heart.

1 SAMUEL 16:7

It was Christmas day. The whole family was gathered. There were presents under the tree waiting to be opened. People were having conversations in different rooms throughout the house. Lucas was only about six months old so he enjoyed watching his older cousins, Teresa and Erin, run and play and have a good time.

We all went into the family room to open the presents. Lucas was really too young to understand what was going on. But if we put a present between his legs, he was able to pull off the bow and eventually, with a little help, rip the paper off.

As we were opening the gifts, someone took one of the bows and put it on Lucas' head. Everyone laughed and said how "cute" he looked. Everyone, that is, except me.

I couldn't help thinking that no son of mine should be getting his picture taken with a *bow* on his head. A baseball cap or a firefighter's helmet, maybe even a cowboy hat! But not a pretty little bow. No son of mine, that's for sure.

Of course, I didn't give my wife's family this "No son of mine" speech. That would have been a quick way to end an otherwise joyful moment around the Christmas tree.

And the thing was, Lucas didn't care. He hardly even noticed. He was just enjoying the people around him. He was still smiling and laughing and having a good time. He was still his regular, bubbly, beautiful self.

I think Lucas lived more closely to the Lord's words to Samuel when Samuel was looking for a king. Samuel was told, "Do not look on his appearance or on the height of his stature, because I have rejected him; for the Lord does not see as mortals see; they look on the outward appearance, but the Lord looks on the heart."

God doesn't judge us by our looks or our height or our hair or our weight or our clothes. God sees beyond this, above this, to another dimension entirely. God sees what goes on inside. God sees into our heart. This is where we are really defined. This is where our values and our personality really live. This is what God is most concerned about.

- **How do you see others?**
- **How do you see your own kids?**
- **How do you see yourself?**
- **Are you able to look on the inside? Are you able to see as God sees?**

A word with God

Loving God, help me to see as you see this coming week. Help me to look on the inside of others and to appreciate the inner beauty that we all share. I pray also that I might see myself as you see me, and focus on my inner heart instead of on my outer appearance. Thank you for loving me on the inside. Amen.

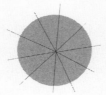

Taking that First Step

"Lord, if it's you," Peter replied, "tell me to come to you on the water."
"Come," he said. Then Peter got down out of the boat, walked on the water
and came toward Jesus.
MATTHEW 14:28–29 (NIV)

There is nothing quite like watching your child learning to walk. First they sit, then they crawl, then they get really brave and pull themselves up to a standing position. From there, they often start to "cruise." Around his first birthday, Lucas started cruising, walking around the room, going from the coffee table to the couch to the chair to the toy box. The whole time he felt safe because he was holding on to something solid.

His next step was to take a few steps between Mom and Dad. I'd get down on the floor and hold him up. Then I'd send him in the direction of Katrina. He'd stumble forward, take a few steps, and then she'd catch him. He was closer to independent walking, but still in the safety of adult arms.

Finally, one day, he decided that it was time to move up the transportation ladder. He would officially make the move from crawling to walking. It was so exciting to see him the day he got up the courage to take those first steps on his own. From then on, whenever he wanted a toy on the other side of the room, he'd prop himself up to his feet, and then scurry to get it with sometimes wobbly little steps.

Those first steps are the toughest. It takes a while to get a feel for it. The child has to trust that when they pick up their foot and then place it back down, they're going to hit solid ground. And as the ground seems to rock back and forth as they go, they've got to trust that they're not going to fall flat on their face. They've got to trust that everything's going to be okay.

Jesus invited Peter to take some pretty dangerous-seeming first steps. Peter was in a boat and called out to Jesus who was walking across the water. He said, "If it's really you, Jesus, tell me to come to you on the water." Jesus encouraged him and said, "Come."

Just as we encourage our kids to take that first step, Jesus encouraged Peter to get out of the boat, to step out onto the water. Have you had to step out of a boat and onto the water lately? Are you looking for the courage and trust that will allow you to take that first step?

These "first steps" happen for us in all kinds of ways. Getting married, having a baby, starting a new job, taking on a project, moving to a new house, trying a new sport or hobby, calling an old friend, mending a bad relationship, going on a big trip – all these are just some of the first steps we take in life. Usually, they require both courage and trust.

It's almost too obvious to say, but we all know that if we don't take those first steps, we never learn to walk. And the only thing more disappointing than falling would be to never make the attempt.

- **What "first steps" are you going to take today?**

A word with God

Dear God, give me the courage to take some first steps this week, knowing that I can depend on you for courage and support. Help me to search if I'm not sure where those steps are leading, but ultimately to trust in you to guide the way. Thank you for encouraging me to get out of the boat! In Jesus' name I pray. Amen.

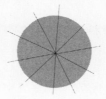

Stuck!

I will call upon the Lord…and so shall I be saved.
PSALM 18:3

As children get a little older, you can let them play on their own a bit more. Lucas usually preferred to play with us, but, though we enjoyed it immensely, there were times when we had to encourage him to do his own thing. It was all part of learning some independence.

One evening, we were in the kitchen cooking some dinner and chatting about the day when we heard Lucas calling from the other room. He wasn't panicking. He wasn't screaming our names. He wasn't crying. He was simply calling out for help.

He did this by repeating the word "stuck." His voice was just loud enough for us to hear, so we knew he wasn't too upset. Faintly, we heard him say "stuck." There was a pause. Then we'd hear it again: "stuck." And then the "stuck's" started coming more quickly and a little more loudly.

By this time, we had come in to the living room where he had been playing and we saw what had happened. Lucas had been pushing his little car that helped him learn how to walk. Somehow, he'd become stuck in a corner between the toy box and the wall and he couldn't get himself out. So he called out for help.

Of course we were happy to help Lucas. It was simply a matter of picking up the little car and turning it around the other way. Then he was on his way again, making tracks.

Sometimes we find that we reach a point in life where we become stuck. Maybe a project isn't going the way we'd hoped. Or perhaps a previous decision isn't turning out the way we'd planned. We might be down about a situation in our life, perhaps a relationship that isn't going anywhere.

As parents, we come to crossroads and face challenges and have our patience tried in ways that leave us saying "Stuck, stuck, stuck!" almost every day. God has given us independence. But just like a parent waiting to be called, God desires to be there for us.

In Jesus Christ, God has come into the world to say "I am with you." And so when we reach the stuck point, maybe even today or tomorrow, we can call out like the psalmist, saying, "I will call upon the Lord and so shall I be saved."

- What are some of your stuck points?
- Would you be willing to call on God to help you through?

A word with God

What a comfort to know that you are with me, dear God. Thank you for your desire to be with me and to help me through all of life – the smooth times and the times when I get stuck. Help me to call on you in confidence and without hesitation, for you are good and your love is sufficient. In Jesus' name I pray. Amen.

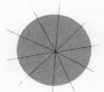

A Heart of Compassion

When Jesus saw the crowds, he had compassion for them,
because they were harassed and helpless, like sheep without a shepherd.

MATTHEW 9:36

I've often underestimated the capabilities of children. I've found that they understand way more than I give them credit for. Who hasn't had a little one repeat something that you didn't even realize you'd said? Children are also able, I've discovered, to endure much more than I thought they could. Whether it's recovering from a fall or hanging in there when it's way past their bedtime, their endurance is amazing.

One day, we discovered another way in which we had underestimated Lucas. It was his ability to feel the sorrow and pain that we were experiencing.

We received a phone call one afternoon from Katrina's mother. She had called to tell us that Katrina's "Granny" from England had just passed away that day. Katrina was extremely upset. She had been very close to her Granny. Granny was 92 years old and until a couple of years prior to her death she had continued to come over to Canada each year for a few weeks. Katrina always made a point of spending some quality time with her. They wrote to each other and even talked on the phone once in a while. And so Katrina couldn't help but show her deep sadness when she heard the news.

However, what surprised us was Lucas' reaction. He became quite subdued. This was not his nature. Usually, he was bubbly and full of life. But after the sad news and Katrina's reaction, he became a different person. He didn't even want to eat. His desire for food, which was also a part of his nature, was nonexistent. And then he got tired and had a late afternoon nap. This was unusual because he rarely slept that late in the day. But on this particular day, he needed a rest.

We'll never know for sure, but I believe that this was Lucas' response to the news we received that day. He may not have understood the reality of what had happened; he didn't even know Granny and certainly didn't understand that this was his great-grandmother. But his little mind and heart *did* seem to recognize that his mommy's heart was sad. And it appeared that her heart became his heart.

In Matthew 9:36, it says, "When Jesus saw the crowds, he had compassion for them, because they were harassed and helpless, like sheep without a shepherd." Can you imagine how the world might be different if God's heart became our heart? Wouldn't we look at people, at all people, a little differently if our hearts beat in time with God's heart?

- **What if we lived with Jesus' heart of compassion?**
- **How might we do that today?**

A word with God

As the creator of life, you, O God, understand the human heart better than any surgeon. Thank you for your compassion and care towards humanity. Wrap your loving arms around nations, communities, families, and individuals who find themselves helpless today. Live in me today so that my heart might beat in time with your compassionate heart. Amen.

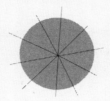

Taste and See

Taste and see that the Lord is good, blessed is the one who takes refuge in God.
PSALM 34:8 (NIV, ADAPTED)

Do you remember how cautious you were with your first child? Everything clean and sterilized, baby-sensitive laundry detergent, and of course, nothing but the most healthy of diets! We were that way, especially when it came to food. No sugar, no suckers, no cake, no ice cream. (Frozen yogurt was our idea of pushing the limit!) We were so careful with Lucas during the first year that he thought unsalted whole wheat melba toast was a cookie!

And then came the day when everything changed. Lucas's first birthday. Maybe it has something to do with seeing your child smear cake all over their face as they stuff huge handfuls into their wide-open mouths. After all, you know it's going to be pretty difficult to deny them this pleasure in the future.

Once the first birthday was over and sugars had been effectively introduced, it was just a matter of time until Lucas got immersed into "Nana's" baking.

My mom is known for her baking. It's in her blood. Both her parents were very able in the kitchen and produced a steady stream of coconut cream pies and molasses cookies. Over the years, my mom's specialty has become her chocolate chip cookies. They're big. They're chewy. They're full of chocolate. Anyone who has ever had one agrees that they're the best.

So perhaps it was natural that I had gotten Lucas pumped up for the day when we would help her make cookies. However, it wasn't until he saw the first batch come out of the oven that he *really* got excited. He watched intently as Nana took the cookies off the trays and placed them on the table. The smell of fresh baked cookies filled the house. We told Lucas that he'd have to wait for a few minutes, until they had cooled. But *finally*, he got to taste these cookies that he'd heard about, looked at and smelled. Oh boy! This sure beat melba toast!

In Psalm 34, the psalmist invites us to leave the fringes, *encourages* us to do more than look from afar. "Dive in!" the psalmist says. "Taste and see that the Lord is good."

This invitation is pretty significant, if we really think about it. It means that God isn't some faraway, distant, outside force. God is One we can feel and taste and see. God is One whom we can relate to, someone to love and be loved by. Through all kinds of people and places and events, we can taste the sweetness of a tender creator who desires the best for humanity.

There's something special about our first taste of God. Life is different. Our experience becomes more rich and full. Joy becomes more real. Important relationships become more important.

- How might you taste more fully the goodness of God?
- Are you open to that goodness moment by moment and day by day?
- What sweetness has God got in store for you today?

A word with God

Open the eyes of my heart, O God, and help me to see your goodness shining through the events of today. May the knowledge of your love enhance all my senses, so that I may fully taste and feel and hear you all around me. Thank you for this gift, and for your desire that we experience life to the fullest. I pray that I will do that, with you. Amen.

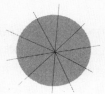

Sharing Our Toys

All the believers were together and had everything in common.
Selling their possessions and goods, they gave to anyone as they had need.
ACTS 2:44–45 (NIV)

It was the most interesting thing to watch. At Lucas' first birthday, I sat back and observed the scene as it played out. Lucas was sitting with Katrina on the floor. He was opening some gifts that our friends and family had brought that day. He would open one gift, set it to the side, and then get ready to take the paper off the next one.

As he did this, his little buddy Will would come along and check out each new toy. Then Will would pick up the toy and take it over to the far corner. I watched him do this three or four times and he always followed the same pattern; he would watch Lucas open a gift, wait till Lucas moved on to the next one, then quietly take the latest gift over to his stash in the corner.

As I observed this, I wondered how long it would take before Lucas realized what was going on. Sure enough, by the time he was about half-way through the gifts, he caught a glimpse of Will walking away with his newest toy. He moved towards Will and *then* he saw all of the other gifts he'd already opened. Okay, I thought, this should be interesting.

Lucas approached Will and I thought he was going to go in for the interception. It looked like an ugly situation. And then, all of a sudden, Lucas looked back at the unopened presents that were still waiting for him. I could almost see the light go on in his head. It was as if he realized he had *lots* of toys and that if Will wanted to enjoy some, why not? (Of course this would be a totally different story if it had been his *second* birthday party!)

What a great lesson, I thought, as I observed and learned from these two toddlers. Will didn't sit in the corner and sulk because it wasn't *his* birthday. He enjoyed it just as if it *was* his birthday. And Lucas didn't become possessive and controlling. He seemed happy to share the wealth.

What a great way to live! Acts 2:44–45 describes this kind of community. "All the believers were together and had everything in common. Selling their possessions and goods, they gave to anyone as they had need."

Reading this, my first thought is that it sounds pretty challenging. But then, if a one-year-old can do it at his birthday party, perhaps I can find a way.

- **Are you able to share your "toys"? Are you able to celebrate when your friends do well? When someone you know gets a raise, do you cheer them on or do you sulk in a corner wishing it was you?**

- And what about the other side of the coin? When you get a new "toy," a big tax return or a financial boost, are you able to share that with others? Have you ever felt the joy of sharing your wealth?

A word with God

Dear God, thank you for all the blessings I enjoy: family, friends, financial wealth, job security…May I see opportunities to share these blessings with others and do it freely and generously, without hesitation, for that is what you desire of us! Amen.

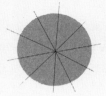

If You Love Me

He said to him the third time, "Simon son of John, do you love me?"…
And he said to him, "Lord, you know everything; you know that I love you."
Jesus said to him, "Feed my sheep."

JOHN 21:17

One night I was giving Lucas a bath and within moments a grand old time turned bad. Lucas loved to try to stand in the bathtub. Trouble was, he'd always slip. Usually Mom or Dad was there to catch him and to tell him that standing was dangerous. Unfortunately, not this time.

After Lucas slipped, there was that long, stressful pause when you wonder if your child will laugh it off or cry incessantly. Even before the fat lip could make its appearance, I knew Lucas was choosing the second option. He began to cry. Loudly.

I shut the bathroom door quickly and started to sing loudly myself in an attempt to mask the sound of Lucas' panicky cry, which broadcast loud and clear, "Mom, why did you leave me with this incapable, unreliable half of the parent species!?"

The louder he cried, the louder I sang "Rubber ducky, you're the one.

You make bath time *so much fun...*"

I finished the bath as quickly as I could. The only problem was that in order to get to Lucas' room I needed to open the bathroom door. And he was still crying loudly. Katrina would surely hear the wails of our hurting child.

I hadn't been in his room for more than two minutes when Katrina came up to see what was happening. Her look said, "If you really, really love me, than you better be sure to take the very best care of our precious son." And in that moment I realized that my responsibility didn't just spring from my love for *my* son, it came from my love for my wife, who also loved *our* son.

Jesus' words to Peter, "If you love me, feed my sheep" call Peter to care for others, and to do it not just out of his love for others, but also out of his love for God.

- Have you ever thought about who Jesus is calling you to love?
- How does your care of others connect with your faith?
- Who might you feed today?
- Who might you love in order that you might more fully love God?

A word with God

Gracious God, forgive me when my ego and pride prevent me from loving others. Your love for me is so great, may I find ways to pass it on to others this day and every day. Help me see that the best way to show my love for you is to love those around me. Amen.

Fishing for People

And he said to them, "Follow me, and I will make you fish for people."
MATTHEW 4:19

One of the most exciting stages of a child's development has to be when they begin to talk. And, of course, our greatest desire comes true when they finally learn how to say our name. It feels wonderful in a way that is difficult to describe.

Lucas had a gift in that he took a keen interest in knowing and saying people's names. He would look at pictures on the fridge and point to people as we said their names. Then he started saying their names himself.

One Easter morning, we went to a sunrise service at church. We were a little late, so we tried to sneak in the back. Within a few seconds of sitting down, Lucas started recognizing people he knew. Being the social butterfly that he was and wanting to exercise his particular gift, he started blurting out their names: "Shistfer" (a.k.a. Christopher), "Teve" (a.k.a. Steve), "Dareene," "Norm," "Peter," and on and on he went. As he said their names, these people turned around and gave him a big smile. The only bad thing was that all this was happening in the middle of a church service. So we took him outside, where he looked in through the glass and continued to call out the names of people he knew.

People were the most important thing in Lucas' life. That's why he loved to say their names. You could say he was in the people business. And even though he wasn't yet two years old, he made people feel important.

God is in the people business. When Jesus calls Simon and Andrew to join him in his work, he is quite clear about what the most important thing is on his agenda: *people*. Knowing that Simon and Andrew have spent their lives fishing, Jesus makes them an offer that they can relate to, but which also expresses what's most important to *him*. He says, "Follow me and I will make you fish for people." Jesus invites them to spend their lives building up, encouraging, and uplifting the most important commodity on the market. Working for the good of other people is the greatest task to which we can offer our time and energy.

- **Who are the people in your life that you would like to put your energy into today? Is there someone you will meet today whose heart you can touch just by knowing and using their name?**

A word with God

To the one who knows my name, help me to be a better steward of my energy, and to direct more towards the people in my life. I am reminded, O God, that in my life people and relationships are the most important things. I pray that I might foster these gifts today, to encourage my friends, to build up my co-workers and to show love to my family. Thank you for Jesus, who modeled how to reach out to others. May I imitate Christ's model today. Amen.

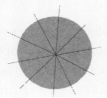

A Special Day

Now listen, you who say, "Today or tomorrow we will go to this or that city,
spend a year there, carry on business and make money."
Why, you do not even know what will happen tomorrow. What is your life?
You are a mist that appears for a little while and then vanishes.

JAMES 4:13–14 (NIV)

For Katrina's 30th birthday I'd arranged a little surprise. I had planned a whole day together just for her and me. It included a trip downtown for lunch at a favorite restaurant of ours, as well as some shopping, some pampering, and then a nice dinner to cap it all off.

She *thought,* when I dropped her off at the gym, that Lucas and I were going to go get some groceries. But instead I went back home, packed up Lucas' stuff and took him to the home of our good friends, the Allins, who had agreed to keep him for the day.

Later, when I showed up back at the gym without Lucas, she knew something was up. We had a great day together. When it was over, we went to pick Lucas up. He had had a good day too. As our friends told us about it, Lucas would periodically interrupt and declare, "Special day! Special day!"

We soon discovered why. Apparently, when Lucas had asked where Mommy and Daddy were, our friends had told him that this was a "special day." It was special because it was Mommy's birthday and she was spending the day with Daddy. It was also special because Lucas and the Allins got to spend a day together.

After we got home, I started thinking about this "special day" thing. Wouldn't it be great if we entered into every day thinking it was special? How wonderful it would be to go to bed each night recognizing that this had been a special day?

Because it really is true. Every day *is* special. Every day is different and unique from the one we lived yesterday and from the one we will live tomorrow. Every day is special because there are always things to be thankful for. There are always things to look forward to.

I realized, "It doesn't have to be Katrina's 30th birthday to be a special day." Every day *can* be a special day. We can *make* it a special day. Try something new. Call an old friend. Enjoy a treat. Take a walk and smell the flowers.

I think the writer of James had a similar idea when he wrote, "Now listen, you who say, 'Today or tomorrow we will go to this or that city, spend a year there, carry on business and make money.' Why, you do not even know what will happen tomorrow. What is your life? You are a mist that appears for a little while and then vanishes."

Life is short – it's too short to not make every day special.

- **How are you going to make today special? Maybe it already is!**

A word with God

Gracious God, today let me see the extraordinary in the ordinary. Your creation is so amazing; surely, each day holds something wonderful for me to see. May I appreciate the works of your hands this special day, and in so doing, make it special for someone else.

Choosing the Most Important

Martha, you are worried and distracted by many things;
there is need of only one thing.

LUKE 10:41

I have always loved mornings. For those who like to hit the snooze button over and over, this may seem a bit strange. But mornings have often been a time of quiet and focus for me. My days can get pretty busy, so the early hours have tended to be my "calm before the storm." This "calm" often included reading or journaling or praying. It was a time to prepare for the day.

Having a child changed that a bit. It was no longer *my* time. It became *our* time. You see, Lucas usually woke up by 6:00 or 6:30 a.m. At first, I tried to keep to my routine and just wake up before him. But that proved difficult, especially on those mornings after I'd gone to bed too late the night before, or happened to be up in the night comforting a crying child (which Katrina will claim was not very often!).

So as happens with many parents, my child became my alarm clock. When Lucas woke up, I woke up. When he was just a baby, I was still able to keep my routine. He would simply sit in his little seat or lie on the floor as I did my thing. But as he became more active, I found *my* time getting shorter and shorter.

One day, I was sitting on the couch journaling while Lucas played in the middle of the room. Lucas came over to the couch where I sat, pulled on my pant leg, and said, "Daddy play?!"

Oh man. What was more important here? To get focused and have some quiet time, or to enjoy some early morning play with my son?

It didn't take me long to figure that one out. The book got put away and I ended up on the floor playing.

I wonder if the "Oh man" I experienced was the same kind of thing that Martha felt when Jesus said to her, "Martha, you are worried and distracted by many things; there is need of only one thing."

Martha's sister Mary had been sitting with Jesus enjoying his company while Martha was busy doing "stuff." When Martha complains to Jesus, this is the message that he offers. You're too busy. You're too task-oriented. Chill. Relax. Breathe.

No doubt there is a time to be a mover and a shaker. There is a time to be busy and to get things done. But surely there's also a time just to enjoy the people in our lives, including our children. And at the end of the day, isn't that what it's all about?

- **What about you? Are you able to choose people over productivity? To leave work at work and to enter fully into that conversation, that family dinner, that time at the park?**

Remember what Jesus said: "There is need of only one thing."

- Who is that "one thing" in your life that needs you?

A word with God

O God, you know us so well that you share in all our moments. Help me to take the time today to follow Mary's example and to enter fully into the moments of the people in my life. Remind me that sometimes the greatest gift I can give to others is my time and my undivided attention.

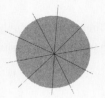

A Wonderful Place

How lovely is your dwelling place, O Lord of hosts!
My soul longs, indeed it faints for the courts of the Lord;
my heart and my flesh sing for joy to the living God.

PSALM 84:1–2

There are places in our lives that hold special memories. Places that excite us, even when we just think about them. Places that make our hearts sing for joy. Places we long to be when life gets rough and we're looking for a break.

One of these places for us has always been "the farm." When I say "the farm," I mean the home of Katrina's parents. They live on a small ten-acre farm just west of Hamilton, Ontario. Over the years it has been a haven for us. As soon as we turn into the driveway, I feel as if I am in another world. I feel more at ease.

Lucas found the farm to be a haven for his own reasons. It was always a place he loved to go. There was Tasha, the new dog, who barked and barked as soon as we drove in. Sometimes this scared Lucas; sometimes it didn't. But it always interested him. He would run around the house looking for Tasha. He loved to throw the ball and watch Tasha run and fetch it. His arms would fly with excitement as he anticipated Tasha's return.

Then there was the piano. Lucas' first move every time he entered the farmhouse was to run into the living room in search of the piano. He would get one of us to sit on the bench with him – Granny was his first choice if she was available – and together we would bang away at the piano keys.

Then there was the little step leading from the kitchen to the hallway where the bedrooms are located. It's not much of a step. I guess that's why it offered a perfect jumping station. Before he could walk, Lucas would crawl up and down, up and down. The step was just small enough that he could make it with ease. Then, when he started walking, he'd stand on the ledge and jump to the main floor, all three inches. Talk about excitement. You'd think he was jumping off a 65-foot cliff into the deep sea.

And, of course, no farm is worth its weight unless it has a tractor. Lucas loved the tractor. He'd watch Grandad from the window, whenever he ventured out on his John Deere. As Lucas got older, he'd come up to the barn saying "tractor, tractor" the entire way. Once he got close enough to touch it, however, he'd back down with his tail between his legs, frightened by Grandad's big toy.

All of this was part of life at the farm. When we called Katrina's parents, Lucas would get on the phone and remember some of these special things that made the farm a warm place for him, even at such a young age. He'd say "Tasha," "tractor," "Dada" (Grandad), "Ranny" (Granny), his excitement mounting as he recalled this special place.

It's good to have places like that. Places we feel warm. Places we find rest. Places we long to be and remember with a smile.

God desires for us to have these kinds of places. Psalm 84 says, "How lovely is your dwelling place, O Lord of hosts! My soul longs, indeed it faints for the courts of the Lord; my heart and my flesh sing for joy to the living God."

Those places where we find God's presence are wonderful places. It can be a farm, where we get to play with a dog and find rest for our busy lives. Or it can be a place of worship where we go each week to open ourselves up to be loved by our Creator and to say my soul longs for you. We know that Christ's presence is there as our hearts sing for joy.

- **Where do you find God's presence? Have you been there lately?**
- **Does your soul long for a visit, to find the peace and rest and joy that place offers?**

A word with God

Thank you, God, for those places where I have found your presence in the past. Thank you that even the memory of them can bring peace and love to my heart. Help me to find a wonderful place today, that I might experience your presence. Amen.

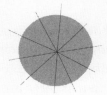

Being Together

For where two or three are gathered in my name, I am there among them.
MATTHEW 18:20

Lucas always loved going to church on Sunday mornings. As soon as we got there, he'd look for two very special people. First, there was Laura, a teenager who frequently babysat for us and who was often at church as early as we were. Because Laura was there early, she'd often spend time with Lucas. They'd play on the piano. They'd find some toys in the nursery. They'd sneak a doughnut from the back. Laura loved Lucas and Lucas loved Laura. He couldn't wait to see her on Sunday mornings.

Then there was Adam, the other special Sunday morning person. Lucas looked forward to seeing Adam for two reasons: Adam played the drums, and he regularly had a rice crispy square for breakfast! For Lucas, this translated into fun making noise on the drums, and sharing a yummy treat with his good buddy. But their connection was about more than that. They always had fun together. They always laughed and played and felt better about life just by being together.

Many Sunday mornings as I was getting prepared, I'd see the three of them sitting together somewhere in the church. There was something special about this weekly gathering for all three of them. I am reminded of Jesus' words, "For where two or three are gathered in my name, I am there among them."

Something wonderful happens when we get together with other people. It can be a team of people who work together on a project. It can be a family reunion. It can be a day spent with our kids. It can be a night out with good friends.

When we gather together with other people, incredible things happen. Our lives fill with joy. We experience a sense of connection. We venture outside of ourselves. Whether we laugh or talk or pray or work or sit quietly together, something special transpires.

What makes it even more special is when we recognize that God is present too. Jesus said, "When you gather in my name, I am there." When we gather with a sense of appreciation and gratitude, God is present. When we gather with the deep passion and life with which Christ lived, God is present. When we gather with others we truly care about, whether it's at the hospital or in the gym or early on a Sunday morning, Jesus' promise comes true. God shows up.

- **Who are you going to be with today?**
- **Are you open to Christ's presence in that gathering?**

A word with God

Dear God, thank you for the people in my life. Thank you for the people I will be with today. Open my eyes so that I can see you in others. May I recognize the beauty of your presence in even my most simple connections with others today. Amen.

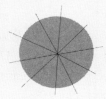

Conky on the Bonky

"But we also rejoice in our sufferings,
because we know that suffering produces perseverance;
perseverance, character; and character, hope. And hope does not disappoint us,
because God's love has poured into our hearts…"
ROMANS 5:3–5 (NIV, ADAPTED)

One day I was with Lucas when he hit his head on something. I don't even remember what it was. It may have been the side of a table. What I *do* remember was his reaction to the incident.

I expected him to get upset. I thought for sure that he would start to cry and come to me looking for some comfort. But that's not what he did.

He rubbed his head and said with a little smile on his face, "Conky on the bonky!" What was this all about? No tears? No crying? No running to Mommy or Daddy? A little shrug, a bit of a rub, a chuckle, and a "Conky on the bonky"?

Lucas had learned this expression from one of our friends, Sharon Nimmo. Apparently, whenever someone bonked their head, Sharon's father would say, "Conky on the bonky." One day when Lucas had bumped his head, before he could decide that he was hurt and start crying, Sharon piped up with this wonderful reaction to a less-than-wonderful situation.

And did it ever work! Even when Lucas hit his head hard, this new saying worked wonders. He would turn to us with a look that said, "Did that ever hurt!" and "Plug your ears cause here comes a big one," and all we had to say was "Lucas, conky on the bonky?"

Quickly, he'd recover, nod his head in agreement, and say back to us, "Conky on the bonky!" Then he'd laugh instead of cry. It was great! This new saying helped Lucas recover and make light of the situation, rather than cry and make a fuss.

How I wish I could do that more. When those little things start to wear on you, wouldn't it be helpful to have a strategy to put them into perspective and lighten up? Rather than getting an ulcer or having an anxiety attack, wouldn't it be better just to say, "Oh well. Conky on the bonky"?

Oops! My stocks just took a turn for the worse. Conky on the bonky. Oh no! The kids spilled all over my clean floor. Conky on the bonky. Aw man! The car needs more work done. Conky on the bonky.

If we could take these life "hits" as well as Lucas learned to take a hit to the head, I've got to think we'd be much better off. I see others roll with life in this kind of way. Nothing could be more inspiring.

In Romans, Paul writes, "But we also rejoice in our sufferings, because we know that suffering produces perseverance; perseverance, character;

and character, hope. And hope does not disappoint us, because God's love has been poured out into our hearts…"

- How do you react to the hits you take in life? Is it the big ones that challenge you most? Or is it the little day-to-day challenges that wear you down?
- How could you react more positively in these situations?
- Can God help you with that?

A word with God

Life is not always easy or smooth. I pray for strength during the difficult moments, to lean on you, dear God, and rest in your love. May it give me perspective and courage to move through the trying times to the good times I know will come. Amen.

Right Back, Mommy!

But we had to celebrate and be glad
because this brother of yours was dead and is alive again:
he was lost and now is found.
LUKE 15:32

There were many times when Lucas was younger that we would have him on our bed as we got him dressed or changed his diaper. Often, we would need to run to his room to get something and the easiest thing to do was to have Lucas stay where he was until we returned.

Katrina would look at Lucas, point her finger in the air, and say, "I'll be right back, Lucas. You stay right there. I'll be right back!"

Lucas didn't forget this experience once he got a little older. One morning as Lucas ran into our bedroom, Katrina started laughing and told me I just had to see his latest trick.

While Lucas stood at the foot of our bed, Katrina said to him, "Lucas, right back?" Lucas thought for a moment and then smiled as he remembered what came next. He pointed his finger in the air, as tiny as it was, and said, "Right back, Mommy, right back."

From then on, whenever he came into our room in the morning and we asked him to go get something, whether it was a toy or a ball, he would first do his "right back" routine. In fact, some days he was so proud of this new trick that he would do it on his own, over and over again. He'd cry, "Right back, Mommy," run out into the hallway, and then come running back into our room with the biggest grin on his face.

To be able to come back brought Lucas great joy. To know that we would still be there and that nothing would have changed brought a smile to his face. What he perhaps didn't know was that we were just as excited as we waited (all two or three seconds!) for his return.

Jesus tells a story about a young man who leaves his parents for a while. Eventually, the young man gets into trouble and decides to return home, even though he's worried about the reception he'll receive. But the young man's father is so excited and happy that his son has returned, he throws him a party (Luke 15:11–32).

God invites us to come "right back" every time we find ourselves out there on our own. Every time we distance ourselves from God, we can find joy in knowing that God will be there and is excited to love us on our return.

- Is there something in your life that has made you feel distant from God?
- Can you trust that God's great love is awaiting your return, regardless of the situation?
- Are you ready to return to those arms of love today?

A word with God

Dear God, there have been many times when I have allowed people, things, and events, to distance me from your love. Thank you for always welcoming me with open arms. Help me to remember that there is nothing I can do that you won't forgive and forget. Thank you for loving me no matter how far away I feel. Help me today to hold you close to my heart. Amen.

How Many Times?

Then Peter came and said to him,
"Lord, if another member of the church sins against me, how often should I forgive?
As many as seven times?"
Jesus said to him, "Not seven times, but, I tell you, seventy times seven ."
MATTHEW 18:21-22

It was a beautiful summer day. The sun was out. There was no wind. The temperature was hot. Fortunately, we were at a friend's house and since they had a pool we officially designated it a "pool day."

As soon as he saw the bright blue water, Lucas couldn't wait to jump in. I put on his bathing suit, jumped in the pool myself, and then turned towards the side of the pool where Lucas was standing. I counted to three: 1, 2, 3, jump! Lucas leapt towards me, his face looking up to the sky, his legs straight as a board, his eyes practically bulging out of their sockets. Seconds later he asked, "More?"

We took bets on how many times Lucas would jump into the pool before he got bored. After about 25 jumps, we realized that he was never going to tire and that the future of this game rested on how many times I was willing to catch him.

Someone once asked Jesus how many times we should forgive a person who wrongs us. When asked if seven times was enough, Jesus responded that it should be 70 times seven.

To me, the best part of this story is that if this is what Jesus *asks* of us, it seems reasonable to conclude that this is what he also *offers* us. In Romans 7:15, Paul says that he keeps doing the very things he doesn't want to do. It's like that with us, too. Sometimes we say things we later wish we hadn't said. Sometimes we miss opportunities to make a positive impact. Sometimes, we disappoint those we love.

And when this happens, we can turn to God, who says, "Seventy times seven." We are forgiven for those things that our very nature draws us into. We are forgiven, again and again and again. God doesn't get bored or tire of this gracious act. The future of this forgiveness that we seek doesn't rest on the limits of God, but rather on the limits of our receptivity.

- Is there something in your life for which you seek forgiveness?
- Is there someone who needs *your* forgiveness?

A word with God

Humble me today, O God, that I might come to you and admit my failures and shortcomings, having confidence in your love and forgiveness. I also pray that with that confidence, I may be able to forgive the person in my life who I feel has hurt me. Help me to truly forgive and love again. In the name of the ever-loving, ever-forgiving Christ. Amen.

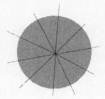

Mommy Tired?

Cast all your anxieties upon him, because he cares for you.
1 PETER 5:7

Sometimes, children pick up on things and respond in ways that just floor you. This happened to us shortly after the birth of our second child, Leah. Katrina had planned to go to a concert with some of her girl-friends just about a week after Leah was born. When she originally said yes to the invitation, she knew she was pushing things a bit, but she was willing to take the chance. Her plan was to take Leah with her. I would stay with Lucas.

On the night of the concert, I came home about an hour before Katrina was supposed to leave. I wanted to hang out with Lucas while she got herself ready.

Katrina went upstairs to get dressed and to pack some things for Leah. Lucas and I spent some time running around the house, but eventually went upstairs where we found Katrina standing in the middle of the bedroom crying. She'd been there for about 20 minutes and hadn't done a thing.

When I asked her what was wrong, she cried even harder. It turned out that she just wasn't sure about a whole lot of things. What should she wear? Nothing really fit right now! What if it rained? Would it get cold down by the lake in Toronto? Could she find something that would allow her to breastfeed easily?

And then there was Leah. What did she need to bring? Would it be too loud for her? How many diapers should she take?

All of this on top of the "hormonal factor" of just having a baby. It was way too much. Katrina slouched down onto the couch and sobbed.

Lucas stopped running from his room to our room, which had been part of the game we'd been playing, and looked at Katrina. He knew something wasn't right.

Many times when Lucas cried we would say, "Lucas must be tired." I guess that explains why he did what he did, which was to go over to the couch and say, "Mommy cry? Mommy tired?" Then he put his head on her shoulder as he sat on her lap for a few minutes.

He was not even two years old, and yet he was caring for his mother. He was able to recognize her need, to be sensitive to the situation and then respond in a way that surprised and touched us deeply.

Children have a way of caring for adults. When we come home cranky after a tough day, they can bring joy that turns us around. When we are stressed, they can help us see our priorities and bring us back to the basics. When we are upset, they can put their head on our shoulder or hold our hand or offer us a hug. Children can offer care that is as good as any adult can offer.

God also offers care. God cares about each and every one of us. God's coming in Jesus Christ says to me that we are never alone. We have a God who understands us and who wants to be part of our lives. 1 Peter 5:7 says, "Cast all your anxieties upon him, because he cares for you."

- What cares are weighing on you today?
- What stresses or heartaches might you be able to share with God, who cares deeply about you?

A word with God

Dear Christ, I pray that I might truly feel your care today. In a society where we are conditioned to keep a stiff upper lip and our troubles to ourselves, teach me to believe in your desire to hear my cares. I bear many burdens – both my own and those of whom I love. I bring all of these to you today. Thank you, for those people in my life who truly care, and for always being a listening ear and a loving heart. Amen.

Joy Comes in the Morning

For his anger lasts only a moment, but his favor is for a lifetime.
Weeping may remain for the night, but joy comes with the morning!
PSALM 30:5 (NIV, ADAPTED)

A ny young parent knows the feeling. It's almost an hour before the alarm is supposed to go off. You are tired because you went to bed later than you had planned. You would give anything for a couple more hours of sleep. But you know you're getting up, because you can hear the calls coming from down the hall.

Lucas was always an early riser. I remember bringing him downstairs with me at 6:30 in the morning, when he was less than six months old. He would just lie there watching me as I worked out in the basement. I'd do a set and then take him through some exercises of his own; I'd bring his feet up to his hands as I counted to ten. He'd smile and giggle as his body went through these new movements.

Then, as he got a little older, he was able to move on his own. We'd come downstairs and play with his toys. Excitement would fill his eyes as he rediscovered his toys after a good night's sleep. I remember the stage when we played basketball in his room at 6:30 in the morning for two weeks straight.

As he got even older, he moved to what we called a "big boy bed." One he could climb out of on his own. So rather than the cries from down the hall, we'd hear him tossing around in his bed; then we'd hear the thump-thump as his feet hit the floor, the bang as he threw open his door, and the pitter-patter as he ran down the hall towards our room. He always came with his blanket and always with a smile. It was as if joy had just entered the room when I heard the words, "Daddy, play toys?" Even though sleep often seemed like a priority, somehow this unmistakable, overflowing, life-giving ball of joy would hit me right in the center of my being.

Psalm 30:5 says, "Weeping may linger for the night, but joy comes in the morning." How true it is! As sure as the sun comes up each day, there is joy each and every morning, if we open ourselves to it. Unmistakable, overflowing, life-giving joy that God offers us through everything from a child's waking up, to a fresh cup of coffee, to a morning walk.

- **What can you find joy in this morning?**
- **Is God offering you a joy that you haven't yet seen?**
- **For whom are you thankful today?**

A word with God

Such joy you offer to me, gracious God. May my eyes be open to see those things around me that I sometimes miss, simply because I don't take the time to look. Thank you for the people in my life with whom I can share your love and your joy. Help me to feel the joy of knowing you, and the peace that comes with that. Amen.

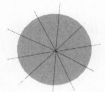

Bedtime Prayers

I thank my God every time I remember you.
PHILIPPIANS 1:3

Most parents develop some sort of routine for their children that takes place before the head hits the pillow and the lights go down. Bedtime can be a wonderful time, for a variety of reasons. Those last few moments before sleep are often incredibly rich and fulfilling. And, of course, there is comfort in knowing that no matter how crazy the day has been, this routine leads to peace and quiet.

I always enjoyed putting Lucas to bed. Often, we would watch sports on the local news before we headed up for a bath. This became so much a part of our routine that Lucas would bring two little chairs and put them in front of the TV once we had finished dinner, just so we could watch together.

The bath was usually a fun time (except for the hair!). Eventually, I would get him to say "bye" to all his bath toys, as a way of signaling that it was time to get out. Then it would be straight to the sink to brush teeth and spit some water (a popular event). Then we'd head to his room to get dried off, have a new diaper and some soft pajamas put on.

Finally, we'd settle into the rocking chair. Lucas would sit on my lap as he held his "blankie" and sucked his thumb. I would read a story or two, and then it would come time for bedtime prayers. Even if there wasn't time for a bath, this last part of the routine always took place.

We would ask Lucas what he was thankful for and he would always name those people who had been in his life that day. Grandparents, parents, friends, cousins, neighbors…the list would go on. Lucas had a deep appreciation for the people in his life. He remembered them as he thought about what it was that he was thankful for.

Philippians 1:3 says, "I thank my God every time I remember you." We interact with people each and every day – people we sometimes take for granted, people we can't imagine living without, people for whom we might want to thank God every time we remember them. There could be no more meaningful bedtime prayer.

- **Who will you thank God for today, and every day?**

A word with God

O God, you have blessed my life with so many people. Thank you for each person who touches my life. Forgive me for the times I may have taken my friends or family for granted. Thank you especially for my children, for the unique and amazing creation they are, and help me to always express my love to them. Amen.

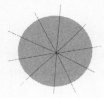

No Higher, Pilot!

I hereby command you: Be strong and courageous;
do not be frightened or dismayed,
for the Lord your God is with you wherever you go.
JOSHUA 1:9

Just before Lucas' second birthday, we flew to Edmonton, Alberta, to visit my brother, Jason, and his wife, Tedra. Though Lucas had been on a plane when he was only seven months old, this would be the first time that he would actually know what was happening. So we decided to prepare him for it by reminding him about this exciting trip coming up. For at least a month prior to our departure, whenever we saw a plane flying overhead, we would say, "Look, Lucas, a plane just like you're going to fly in." He was excited about this, right up until we got to the airport.

We were standing at those floor-to-ceiling windows watching the planes taxi in. When Lucas discovered that this was the plane he was going to be traveling on, he started crying and shouting, "No plane, no plane!" We diverted this very emotional reaction with some French fries and somehow convinced him that going on this plane wouldn't be so bad.

By the time we were ready for takeoff, we had Lucas thinking that going really fast would be a pretty cool thing to do. He was back on board. We were on an aisle seat, so if we leaned far enough into the center of the plane we could actually see into the cockpit where the pilots sat. It was not hard to persuade Lucas to yell as the plane started down the runway, "Go faster, pilot, go faster!" This seemed to give him a sense of control. The pilot was doing as he requested!

Suddenly, as we began to fly higher and higher Lucas looked a little worried. He sensed that he was losing control over this thing and he quickly changed his tone. He leaned into the center of the aisle and looked towards the pilot just as before. Only this time he yelled, "No higher, pilot, no higher!"

Of course, the plane went higher and faster and eventually we landed in Edmonton and everything was fine. Though Lucas entered this new experience with great fear and trepidation, he eventually realized that he had no choice but to trust the pilots and enjoy the flight.

As we go through life, there are times when we feel out of control. There are times when we look at a project or a phone call or a relationship or a situation with fear and trepidation – times when we want to yell, "No higher, pilot, no higher!"

Perhaps what we need to do is simply trust the pilot and enjoy the flight.

In the Old Testament, Joshua, the leader of the Israelites, comes across a situation that has him shaking with fear. God has called him to lead the people into the Promised Land and he finds himself saying, "No higher."

God's response is clear: "Be strong and courageous; do not be frightened or dismayed, for the Lord your God is with you wherever you go."

- **What things in your life might you be able to entrust to God, so that you can better "enjoy the ride"?**

A word with God

Gracious God, my most trustworthy pilot, help me to remember that you are with me in all that I do. Give me the courage to face each situation with confidence in myself and in you. Today, allow me to part from my fear just a little, and increase my trust a lot, so that I might find joy in each experience, the joy that you desire me to have. Thank you for being a loving guide. Amen.

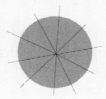

Crazy

This, the first of his miraculous signs, Jesus performed at Cana in Galilee.
He thus revealed his glory, and his disciples put their faith in him.

JOHN 2:11

If it is fair to say that Lucas was excited about his plane ride, he was even more excited about visiting his aunt and uncle who lived so far away. They, of course, went out of their way to make every moment memorable.

One day, Lucas went for a drive with his uncle Jason. By the time they came back, they had invented a special little game. Jason would say the word "crazy." Except he didn't just *say* it. He said it with so much enthusiasm and life, he made those five letters seem like 20: "C-r-a-a-a-a-a-z-y." He also shook his head from side to side for even greater effect.

Jason would initiate this game by saying "C-r-a-a-a-a-a-z-y" and Lucas would respond in exactly the same way. Now it was kind of funny when Jason did it. But when Lucas did it with his big, infectious smile and those sparkling eyes, we all ended up rolling on the floor with laughter. It was one of those things you have to see for yourself to truly appreciate.

Upon investigation, we heard how it all got started. Jason and Lucas had been in Jason's Explorer. Jason had used his power window button to put the windows down, and as the air blew in, he shook his head and let loose: "C-r-a-a-a-a-z-y." Of course, Lucas mimicked him, with even more exuberance as the wind blew in his face. The "crazy game" had begun.

It looked like it felt good for both of them, each time they played the game. It even felt good just to watch them.

It's great to let our hair down sometimes. It feels refreshing and brings new life to let go and have fun and do something that's a little crazy. It's good for our kids and it's good for us. It does something to us that rejuvenates our spirit.

I think that God appreciates these "crazy" moments too, when we step outside the busyness and seriousness of life. In fact, in scripture there are many times when Jesus leaves a situation or says something to lighten the mood. His first miracle was to turn water into wine at a wedding celebration (John 2:1–11)! Now if that doesn't spell fun, what does?

- Have you had any crazy moments lately?
- Is there anything you can do to create some? Do you need to? Do you ever find yourself taking life too seriously?

Before we get too serious here, maybe we should simplify our thinking. Perhaps just reflecting on a humorous moment that has been part of your life recently would be enough work for today. Was it something you read? Something you heard on the radio? Something your child did or said? A silly mistake you made? Enter into the moment and enjoy it. You may even want to tell someone else about it as a way of sharing the joy.

A word with God

Thank you, God, for being a God of joy! As I think of you today, may my smile be a little wider and my eyes a little brighter. Help me to go a little "crazy" today, and to look for opportunities to turn my water into celebratory wine! Amen.

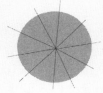

Crocodile Tears

They will hunger no more, and thirst no more;
the sun will not strike them, nor any scorching heat;
for the Lamb at the center of the throne will be their shepherd,
and he will guide them to springs of the water of life,
and God will wipe away every tear from their eyes.
REVELATION 7:16-17

One day I dropped Lucas off at the nursery. As I *tried* to leave, he started crying. Tears streamed down his little face. I hated to leave him. I felt horrible as I left the room. All I could see, running through my mind, was my little man, so very sad. Was I being a bad parent?

Later on, when I picked Lucas up, I asked the woman who had been with him how long he had cried. "Oh," she said, "those were just crocodile tears."

I had never heard that term before. Crocodile tears? She explained that crocodile tears are those big tears that children are very adept at creating on the spot. They come fast. They rest on those big fat baby cheeks, like water drops on a freshly waxed car, just sitting there for Mom and Dad to see. But they don't last long.

This woman told me that Lucas stopped crying less than a minute after I left him. He'd been faking me out with his very own crocodile tears.

I'd like to think that crocodile tears are more than our children trying to put one over on us. It seems to me that they probably do, for a few brief moments, feel genuinely sad about the situation. Maybe they're afraid. Perhaps they really do love us and even though they know that ultimately they're going to be all right, our leaving brings a sense of loss.

But then someone cares for them. Someone assures them it's going to be okay. A favorite toy gets put before them and they realize that there's way too much life to be lived to be sad for long.

The same thing happens to us, if we're honest about it. Most of us find ourselves crying, sad, down, sulking, hurt, and cranky, about things that in the grand scheme of life aren't necessarily that important. And even if the cause is of a more serious nature, most of us come to realize that regardless of the loss that has brought our tears, there really is too much life to be lived to be sad for too long.

The Bible speaks of a God who desires to wipe our tears away. God has a vision in which our sadness and brokenness is replaced with a new way of life. Revelation 7:16–17 says, "They will hunger no more, and thirst no more…and God will wipe away every tear from their eyes."

- What are the causes of your tears these days? How real are they?
- When you look at the bigger picture, is there any chance you're crying crocodile tears?
- Either way, are you able to open yourself up to a God who wants to wipe your tears away? Can you find hope in the future?

A word with God

Sometimes it's easy to become overwhelmed with the small details of life, and the tears flow. Other times, life throws painful blows, and once again the tears flow. Help me today, O God, to take these tears and turn them into rivers of hope. Amen

Finally Sleeping

Come to me, all you who are weary and burdened, and I will give you rest.
Take my yoke upon you and learn from me, for I am gentle and humble in heart, and
you will find rest for your souls.
MATTHEW 11:28–29 (NIV)

You know those times when you wonder whether or not your child is *ever* going to fall asleep? Those times when you try and try and try, and still their eyes refuse to close. Maybe it's in the middle of the night. Maybe it's when you're visiting friends for the evening and you're waiting for the kids to fall asleep before you have dinner. Maybe it's an afternoon and you've been counting on them to sleep so that you can nap too. Or maybe it's on a plane…

That's when it happened to us. We were traveling to Alberta to see my brother. The plan was simple: after dinner, we'd put Lucas' pajamas on, give him his "blankie," read a few books, and then he'd fall asleep in my arms.

The first part of the plan worked fine. It was the falling asleep part that didn't work so well. Lucas nestled down initially. He held his "blankie" close to his cheek and put his head down on my chest. But then someone would walk by and he'd poke his head up to see what was going on.

Eventually, he settled down and appeared to be on his way to dreamland. But there was one last phase to go, which involved Lucas rolling from side to side, like a dog doing circles before lying down! This went on for a good five minutes. And then finally, he stopped.

What a relief! Even better, after all that work, he looked so peaceful. One of the best feelings in the world comes from looking in on your children when they are sleeping. Sometimes, their little bodies are curled up in a ball. Sometimes you find them with their limbs spread out in all different directions. Maybe their head is at the bottom of the bed.

And as you stand over them in the darkness, you can't help but experience a deep peace. You can't help but think how beautiful and wonderful they are, how lucky you are to have these precious lives in your care.

God loves to see us find rest, as well. When we're busy and our plates are full, God invites us to rest. Jesus says in Matthew 11:28, "Come to me, all you who are weary and burdened, and I will give you rest."

Most of us like to keep busy. Often, we feel guilty if we *aren't* doing something. But God wants to give us rest so that we might be renewed. When God looks at us and sees us resting, God gets the same wonderful feeling we get when we look at our children as they sleep.

- Can you accept Jesus' invitation to rest?
- What do you need a break from these days?
- How might you find some rest?

A word with God

God of rest, help me to quiet myself and to feel your presence, knowing that this is as valuable a task as anything else I may have to do today. Help me to leave my burdens with you, so that I may find true rest in my soul. Amen.

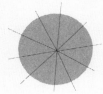

Where'd That Come From?

Therefore be imitators of God, as beloved children, and live in love,
as Christ loved us and gave himself up for us.

EPHESIANS 5:1–2

Lucas and I used to spend lots of time in the garage. Because we had a small driveway, the garage was a good place to play.

One day we were kicking a ball back and forth to each other when one of his kicks happened to go past me. I turned to get the ball and as I did I heard, "SCOOORES!" I looked back to see Lucas with his arms up in the air, as high as they would go, as he continued to yell "SCOOORES!" His face was red and his eyes were practically popping out of his head.

After I picked myself up off the garage floor from laughing so hard, I grabbed Lucas and went inside to show Katrina. "Hey, Katrina, you've got to see this! Watch."

I passed Lucas the ball. He promptly kicked it by me and again threw his arms in the air and yelled "SCOOORES!" Now we were both laughing at Lucas' newest expression.

The question we started to ask each other was, "Where did that come from?" Then, one afternoon, we were picking Lucas up from his caregiver, Darlene. As I made my way downstairs to get Lucas, I saw that he was playing ball with Darlene's son Christopher, who was eight years old.

Christopher kicked the ball past Lucas and, without a moment's hesitation, threw his arms up in the air and yelled, "SCOOORES!" His face was red and his eyes were practically popping out of his head.

Aha! So that's where it came from! Christopher was a few years older than Lucas and that made him a natural role model. Many times when Lucas did things we hadn't seen before, or said words we'd never heard before, we knew where they came from. They came from his big buddy Christopher.

Our children look for people to model their lives after. They will repeat words they hear us say. They will react to situations the same way we do. They will often take on similar attitudes to those we take on. Our choices and decisions about how we live day by day and moment by moment no longer affect just us. Once we become a parent, we are imitated and our every action influences the actions of others.

The question many of us ask is, "Who can *we* imitate?" The apostle Paul says, "Therefore be imitators of God, as beloved children, and live in love, as Christ loved us and gave himself up for us." Paul offers the way of Jesus and the life that he lived as a model we can follow.

Modeling ourselves after God will benefit our children in some really great ways. We will offer them patience, for God is patient with us. We will offer them mercy and forgiveness, because God extends mercy and forgiveness to us. We will bring them hope and encouragement, because God wants to fill us with these as well. And perhaps most importantly of all, if we live our lives in God's way, we will show our children a love that is unconditional and without end, because that is how God loves us.

If our children can grow up to yell "I am loved!" as loudly and with as much energy as Lucas yelled "SCOOORES!" then we'll know we've done something right!

- Do you see yourself in your children?
- Are you happy with what you see?
- In what ways could you tune up the image your children are looking towards for guidance?

A word with God

Our example is so important, O God, and we desire to be a good model for our children. Help me to follow the example of Jesus, who portrayed an image of unconditional love, forgiveness, patience, zest for life, and wise decision-making. Help me today, and every day, to follow more closely in his footsteps. Amen.

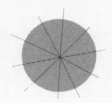

Don't Worry

Do not worry about anything,
but in everything by prayer and supplication with thanksgiving
let your requests be made known to God.
And the peace of God, which surpasses all understanding,
will guard your hearts and your minds in Christ Jesus.

PHILIPPIANS 4:6-7

You wouldn't think that sitting on the couch with your two-year-old child while watching an early morning video could be a stressful thing. It's not like it was a horror movie or anything. Rather, it was Winnie the Pooh!

As harmless as the story seems, however, there was one part that had Lucas on the edge of his seat and terribly frightened every single time. He would cry "Pooh! Pooh!" as he drew himself closer to the television. Then he'd look at me as if to say, "How can you just sit there, Daddy? Do something!"

It was the scene where Pooh uses a balloon to float up into a tree. His destination is a bee's nest and his goal some honey for his bottomless tummy. Somehow, the balloon pops and, as the air comes out of it, Pooh goes flying. Up, up, up, he travels into the sky. And inevitably, Lucas would become terribly worried for his little friend, Pooh bear.

I would do my best to comfort Lucas. I'd move closer and wrap my arm around him. Then I'd assure him that Pooh was going to be all right. "Don't worry, Lucas, don't worry. Pooh is going to be okay." Eventually, Lucas would calm down.

I can't say that I ever worried about Pooh, really. But I certainly get concerned about other people in my life. And just like Lucas, my concern is for people I care deeply about and who, for whatever reason, are at a place in life where they seem to be floating through the air with some uncertainty about the future.

When my brother moved out west years ago, I worried about him. When my dad was in the hospital and had to undergo emergency surgery, I worried about him. When Katrina became overwhelmed with life and struggled with some major decisions about her future career, I worried about her. Do you ever have these kinds of concerns for the people you care about? Do you ever wish there was someone sitting beside you, wrapping their arm around you and saying "Don't worry, it's going to be okay"?

The apostle Paul reminds us that we *do* have One who plays this role in our lives. "Do not worry about anything, but in everything by prayer and supplication with thanksgiving let your requests be made known to God. And the peace of God, which surpasses all understanding, will guard your hearts and your minds in Christ Jesus."

If you're worried about those you care about, try to envision this: There is One who sits on the couch with you. There is One who shares your burden. There is One who can assure you and encourage you and offer you hope. There is One who can replace your worry with peace.

- **What worries do you have that you could share with God today?**

A word with God

Gracious God, thank you for this reminder that I can share my worries with you. Help me to bring them to you today, and to leave them with you, trusting in your promise that you can give me a peace that goes beyond my understanding. I long to feel you beside me and to experience your assurance and comfort. Amen.

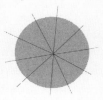

Drive?!

David and all the house of Israel were dancing before the Lord with all their might, with songs and lyres and harps and tambourines and castanets and cymbals.
2 SAMUEL 6:5

There was a period when every time we drove into our townhouse complex Lucas would express a deep desire to drive our car. He expressed this desire in a word that was a question and a whine and an enthusiastic statement all rolled into one. As our little red Tercel pulled into the driveway, Lucas would call out to us from his car seat in the back: "Driiive?!"

Lucas loved to sit on one of our knees and pretend that he was driving. He would grab hold of the steering wheel and turn corners at record speeds. We would pretend to visit various people, say hello, then drive off again. He would play with various knobs that changed the radio station or put the windshield wipers on. He would open the glove compartment and take things out. And, he would do this for as long as we were willing to sit with him.

Now, I kind of knew that this wasn't the best parenting decision I'd ever made. I knew that a car was not a toy. I knew that the neighbors likely looked at us and said to each other, "Can you believe they're letting that little boy do that." I could even hear my own parents' voices in the back of my mind, saying, "We would never have let *you* do that!"

Even though almost everything about this little ritual said it was wrong, there was one thing that kept drawing me to say yes – the pure joy that my son received from this simple experience. What's more, Lucas' joy somehow bubbled over into me, so that I almost couldn't wait for him to say, "Driiive?!"

King David and his friends expressed this kind of joy in their own way, as we read in 2 Samuel: "David and all the house of Israel were dancing before the Lord with all their might, with songs and lyres and harps and tambourines and castanets and cymbals."

- **Have you experienced sheer joy with others lately?**
- **Is it time to do something a little out of the ordinary?**
- **What or who makes your heart sing and dance with joy? Why not do something to celebrate life today?**

A word with God

Dear God, give me the inspiration to do something fun today – to experience joy and to not be quite so serious. Help me to remember and to try some of the simple pleasures that gave me so much joy as a child – walking in the park, getting an ice cream, going roller skating. May I find some way of rejoicing in your love this day. Amen

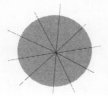

Excited or Afraid?

*Trust in the Lord with all your heart and
lean not on your own understanding;
in all your ways acknowledge God and God will make your paths straight.*
PROVERBS 3:5–6 (NIV, ADAPTED)

One evening, Katrina was at home with Lucas when they had some visitors. Our good friend Peter and his son Alex were out walking a friend's dog and they decided to drop by on their way. They knew Lucas would be excited to see the dog.

When they came to the door, Katrina called Lucas and told him that he had a very special visitor. Lucas was so excited that he could hardly speak. He was also so afraid that he wouldn't let go of Katrina.

Lucas was often this way with dogs. When he was a baby and we walked him in the stroller, he'd get very excited whenever he saw a "doggie" from far away. He'd flap his arms up and down and kick his legs. Once the dog got closer, however, it would be a different story. He'd become shy and nervous and pull away from the dog.

On this particular evening, Lucas had both reactions. And so, as he held tightly to Katrina, he also reached out and touched the dog. The excitement factor won out as he moved beyond his fear.

It became obvious that Lucas was glad he'd taken this step, even though he had been afraid, because he laughed and giggled and smiled.

There are many times when I feel like Lucas did when he encountered dogs. I make countless decisions and take countless actions that leave me feeling both excited *and* afraid at the same time. As I think of the potential and possibilities involved in a new course of action, my heart beats a little faster as the adrenaline flows. But I also feel anxiety. What if it doesn't work out? Will it be too much work? Is this the right thing to do?

It can be a decision regarding our family. Are we going to have more children? Should we move to a bigger home? Is this a good financial decision for us? It can be a decision regarding work. Can I start a new project? Am I hiring the right person? Should I accept that job offer?

Most new things in life seem to inspire a blend of excitement and fear within us. The real question must then be this: Will we let the fear and worry paralyze us? Or will we allow the exciting possibilities to be played out?

Proverbs 3:5–6 says, "Trust in the Lord with all your heart and lean not on your own understanding. In all your ways acknowledge God and God will make your paths straight." Sounds like a good idea to me.

- What excites you these days?
- Are fears holding you back? If you lived out these words from Proverbs 3 and invited God into all areas of your life, what impact would it have on your life?

A word with God

Help me to trust in you today and to acknowledge the part you play in my life. I want to follow your ways, O God, which sometimes take me in directions that I fear. I pray that you will give me the courage to move past my fear and take the next step, whatever it may be, so that I may experience the excitement that comes from expanding my horizons! Amen.

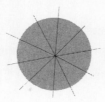

Getting Sidetracked

For you make me glad by your deeds, O Lord; I sing for joy at the works of your hands. How great are your works, O Lord, how profound your thoughts!
PSALM 92:4–5 (NIV)

One day when Lucas and Katrina were on their way to the park across the field from our house, they took a shortcut. Except that it didn't really end up being much of a shortcut. It was more of a sidetrack. They never *did* make it to the park.

Instead, they ended up on a dirt trail. Normally, the route to the park was along a paved path that got you from point A to point B. But this old dirt trail had all kinds of interesting things that made it almost impossible to keep going without stopping to take it all in.

The experience was like taking the scenic route rather than the expressway, like cooking a nice meal instead of popping a frozen dinner into the microwave, like reading the whole book rather than just skimming the back cover.

Sometimes it's good to get sidetracked. For Lucas, it meant he got to enjoy the beauty of the world around him. It didn't matter that he never made it to the park, because there were rocks to pick up and look under. There were long pieces of grass to pull on and wrap around his hand. There were sticks to collect and carry in his pocket. There were flowers to smell. There were bugs and insects to bend down and observe and even talk to. There were all kinds of things that were worth missing the park for. Getting sidetracked, at least on this particular day, was the way to go.

Some days we would do well to get a little more sidetracked. There's so much beauty and wonder in the world around us, it's a shame to push through our day with blinders on.

Why not stop and take in the sunrise on the way to work? Why not take the time to really hear how your colleague's weekend was? Why not get sidetracked from your desk at lunchtime and go for a walk? Why not break from your household activities long enough to step outside and breathe in life for a few moments?

A little less focus and busyness and a little more wonder and awe might be good for us. The psalmist had the right idea when he wrote, "For you make me glad by your deeds, O Lord; I sing for joy at the works of your hands. How great are your works, O Lord, how profound your thoughts!"

- **What are some things you might allow yourself to be sidetracked by today?**
- **What would inspire you to sing for joy?**

A word with God

As I get on with this day, O Lord, help me to be sidetracked by you. Let me be open to your leading and notice some of the little things that are easily ignored. Thank you for such a vast and wonderful creation, and for the wonderful relationships with which you have blessed me. May these be more my focus today! Amen.

Happy with Little

For I have learned to be content with whatever I have.
I know what it is to have little, and I know what it is to have plenty.
PHILIPPIANS 4:11–12

It was one of those drives that just wasn't going well. Our little red Toyota Tercel didn't have air conditioning, and it was *hot!* Lucas was in the back and he was *not* happy! We were on our way back to Ontario from Lansing, Michigan, where we'd been visiting Katrina's sister. Though it had been a great visit, there were moments as the sweat dripped down our backs, and our legs stuck to the hot seats, and Lucas cried with an impressive constancy, that I doubted if we'd ever make the trip again.

And then we saw our oasis. As we crossed the bridge over into Sarnia, Ontario, we spotted a beach just off to our left. We looked at each other and knew that no vote was needed. We were going to stop, go for a swim, and try to gain back some sanity.

We all went in the water for a few minutes. I don't know that water ever felt more refreshing. Lucas played on the beach, running away from the waves as they came into shore. He laughed. We laughed. It was so much fun just to be able to let off some steam after being cooped up in the car.

After a bit, we got changed and even the clothes we'd been wearing felt better after swimming. They felt comfy and clean.

Then we bought some French fries from a chip truck. After loading them with ketchup and salt, we sat by the car and looked out over the water as we ate.

Pretty simple stuff, but for some reason it all added up to a very memorable experience. To this day, whenever I drive over that bridge, I think fondly of those few moments spent on that beach. In fact, if someone even *mentions* Sarnia, I am overcome with good feelings, as images of that well-timed stop float through my memory. I find there are few moments in life when I can say I am truly content, but this was one of them.

In Paul's letter to the Philippians he writes, "Actually, I don't have a sense of needing anything personally. I've learned by now to be quite content whatever my circumstances. I'm just as happy with little as with much, with much as with little" (*The Message*, Eugene H. Peterson).

Paul had a good idea. I don't think he ever spent a hot day driving in a little car with a child crying in the back, but I do know that he had a less-than-easy life. And yet he'd learned to find happiness in simple pleasures and to be content with what he had.

How my life would be better if I could do this consistently. How much richer each day would be if I were able to find in it those many opportunities for contentment.

- **When have you experienced true contentment?**
- **What opportunities for a contented moment might you find today?**

A word with God

Thank you, most gracious God, for those little graces, for those moments when life gets put into perspective and we experience gratitude that touches the core of our being. Whether it's a sunset or a smile, a new insight or a special memory, may we find on this day and in this moment a renewed sense of contentment in those everyday, simple pleasures with which you surround us all the time. Amen.

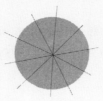

He Just Knows

For you created my inmost being; you knit me together in my mother's womb…
when I was woven together in the depths of the earth,
your eyes saw my unformed body.
PSALM 139:13–16 (NIV)

One day I picked up Lucas from our caregiver's home. I happened to have an old Tim Hortons (our local doughnut shop) coffee cup in the front of the car. As we were driving along, Lucas suddenly said, "timbits?" I realized that he had recognized the coffee cup from Tim's and immediately assumed I had little round treats to go with it! Once I stopped laughing, I informed him that the cup was from earlier that day.

From that day on two things happened. If I went through the drive-thru with Lucas in the back, it became almost impossible not to get some timbits. And I learned to throw out my old cups right away so we wouldn't have this intelligent, timbit-craving toddler begging for one of his favorite snacks.

I couldn't believe that he recognized and remembered the cup, let alone make the association that he did: where there's a coffee cup, there's got to be some doughnuts. Obviously, he'd been to these fine establish-ments often enough that he knew the routine. And he loved timbits enough to pay attention.

God is like that, too. God is aware of far more than most of us real-ize. God recognizes us in mysterious ways that are almost beyond our comprehension. God knows our innermost thoughts, our deepest fears, our heaviest hurts, and our biggest dreams. God knows us so intimately, because God formed our very being.

Psalm 139 says, "For you created my inmost being; you knit me to-gether in my mother's womb...When I was woven together in the depths of the earth, your eyes saw my unformed body." As our Creator, as the One who put us together, God knows us and understands us.

When we find ourselves feeling as if there's a wall between us and God, we might want to remember this psalm and how close to us God really is. Most of us have times in our lives when we'd like to connect with God, but nothing happens. Perhaps we want to pray, but we're not sure how. We might be so upset and angry, that we're not even sure where to start. Maybe we feel unworthy.

The One who put us together is able to break through all of our barriers. Paul wrote about this in his letter to the Romans: "Likewise the Spirit helps us in our weakness; for we do not know how to pray as we ought, but that very Spirit intercedes with sighs too deep for words" (Romans 8:26).

God not only recognizes us, God recognizes our sighs, and our groans, and our very breath.

- **What is God recognizing in you today?**

A word with God

Dear God, it is wonderful that you know me so intimately, yet I sometimes feel so distant. Thank you for knowing my needs even without my speaking them. I pray that I might be able to open myself up once again and share these things with you. How wonderful you are; how wonderful is your love for me. Thank you for your Spirit, who is always with me. Amen.

Hope for the Future

For I am about to create new heavens and a new earth; the former things shall not be remembered or come to mind. But be glad and rejoice forever in what I am creating; for I am about to create Jerusalem as a joy, and its people as a delight.

ISAIAH 65:17–18

One day we were looking after our nieces Teresa and Erin. Truth is, there wasn't much to looking after them because they just played with Lucas. They were both older than him and they treated him almost like a toy.

On this particular day, they were playing dress-up. Now this was during a period of his life when Lucas really didn't like to put on his winter coat, hat, and mitts. So when I saw Teresa and Erin dressing him up in all this stuff, I thought, "Let's see how long this lasts."

A few minutes later, I came back for a second look and he was *still* tolerating their efforts. I couldn't believe it. What was going on? Lucas? Letting his cousins dress him up? Are you kidding me?

Then I found out *why* he was enduring this somewhat painful procedure. Teresa and Erin had promised him that he could go outside when they were done. Lucas *loved* to go outside. He loved the fresh air and the freedom. If he was cranky about something, all you had to say was, "Lucas, want to go outside?" and he would immediately be happy. The promise Teresa and Erin made allowed him to stick with the program, even though it was far from his favorite activity.

Sometimes in life we are forced to endure things that are extremely challenging: the loss of a loved one, a relationship breakdown, bouts of depression, unsatisfactory working conditions... We look at ourselves and we look at others in these situations and we say, "Are you kidding me?"

How do we endure? How do *others* survive? What's the secret to keeping your chin up? Where does one find the strength to continue in the midst of trying circumstances?

The writer of Isaiah says, "For I am about to create new heavens and a new earth; the former things shall not be remembered or come to mind. But be glad and rejoice forever in what I am creating; for I am about to create Jerusalem as a joy, and its people as a delight."

The hope of this promise can be the difference between enduring and giving up. On those really bad days when life seems to be caving in on us, this promise of new things can be key to our survival. We will get through. Outside awaits.

- **What are you trying to endure these days?**
- **Are you able to find solace in the kind of promise we read about in Isaiah?**

A word with God

Gracious God, as I think of those things that I have had to endure and am enduring, I long to feel the comfort of your promises. I pray for your strength and courage for myself, and for others I know who need these things as well, as we all face the trials of life. I look ahead with hope that all will be good again, and that all will be as you intend it to be. Amen.

Giving Away Roses

Some give freely, yet grow all the richer…
PROVERBS 11:24

You would have thought he was carrying a million-dollar check the way he walked up her driveway. His face beamed. His eyes sparkled. This was an exciting mission that he was thrilled to be a part of.

It was Darlene's birthday. Darlene was Lucas' daily caregiver. She wasn't just a "babysitter." She was a playmate. She was a friend. She was a second mother. She was his biggest fan. Even at age two, Lucas knew the special place that Darlene had in his life. And, somehow, he understood, in his own way, the gift of giving to someone else.

And so to give Darlene a rose on her birthday was a pretty big moment for him. This beat opening Christmas gifts. It was way more fulfilling than getting gifts on *his* birthday. This was an opportunity to give to someone else.

We walked up to the door and rang the bell. No answer. No one home except for Sally the dog. Disappointed? No way. Nothing was going to stop this gift from getting through. Nothing was going to take away the joy of this gift.

So we opened up the mailbox, lifted Lucas up, and in went the rose. Face still beaming. Eyes still sparkling. Smile still full. Mission accomplished. Gift given.

Lucas didn't need to see Darlene receive his birthday offering in order to experience the meaning of giving. I'm sure she gushed when she got home. I'm sure she felt like picking him up and hugging him. I'm sure she said to herself, "What a precious gift, this rose and this boy." But he didn't need to see or hear or know any of that in order to receive the joy of giving.

Without even realizing it, Lucas had lived out Jesus' words, "It is more blessed to give than to receive," and made them a reality. He didn't do it to teach someone a lesson. He didn't do it as an experiment. He did it because it just made sense in his little – make that big – heart.

Why not try it today. Give something to someone without any expectations or strings attached whatsoever. It doesn't need to be a million dollars. "Roses" come wrapped in smiles and compliments and encouraging e-mails. Roses come as courteous drivers, as driveways shoveled for neighbors, as doughnuts brought in to the office…

God was right. It is in giving that we truly receive.

- **Experienced the joy of giving lately?**
- **Can you give without getting a thank you?**
- **What "roses" might you hand out today?**

A word with God

In a world that emphasizes getting, help me today to focus on giving, dear God. Help me to give of my time, my patience, my good mood, and my good deeds, for in giving we receive more than we could ever imagine. Open my eyes to the opportunities to give today. Amen.

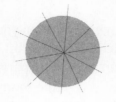

It's All Good

God saw all that God had made, and it was very good.

GENESIS 1:31

It was one of those perfect moments you wish you had taken a picture of so it could be blown up, put in a frame, and hung proudly on the wall for all to see. That didn't happen, but the scene is engraved in my mind and on my heart as one I'll always hold dear, though it's not easy to explain why.

Lucas was holding hands with his granddad as they walked towards the barn. It had something to do with being at the farm, and with the old barn, full of adventure and new experiences. It had something to do with the fact that up to that point Lucas had been reluctant to leave us and go with anyone. It had something to with the connection of those hands. There was a special trust that, though it was unspoken, was clearly present.

We watched from the window. It was a moment when all seemed good and right with the world.

Do you have similar moments etched in your mind and on your heart? Was it a moment spent watching a waterfall, or a sunset or a rainbow? Was it a moment on vacation with your parents growing up? Maybe it was your child getting out of bed in the morning and coming into your room, standing right beside your bed and saying, "Hi Mommy, hi Daddy." What are some special moments for which you find yourself eternally grateful?

The first chapter of Genesis, the first book of the Bible, offers a story of creation. In the midst of all the details regarding the day-by-day order of events, there is something that is even more relevant and meaningful. Over and over again, the story describes God's reaction to the beauty of this world. It's simple, yet profound. It was the reaction we had when we watched Lucas walk to the barn with his granddad. God watched over the unfolding beauty of creation "and God saw that it was good."

What a gift these moments are, when we feel the wonder and beauty of life, when we can say, even if only for the moment, "All is good."

- Where might you be able to look today and say, "All is good"?
- Are you open to the experience?

A word with God

Loving God, in a world where there seems to be so much that is bad, help me to see the good that is also present. Thank you for healthy relationships, for positive experiences, and for the beauty of the earth. Keep those things present in my mind today. Amen.

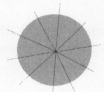

It's Good to See You!

When he was still a long way off, his father saw him.
His heart pounding, he ran out, embraced him, and kissed him.
LUKE 15:20 (*THE MESSAGE*, EUGENE H. PETERSON)

One of the best parts of my day was when I would fetch Lucas from Darlene's house after work. It wasn't that I worried about him. Darlene gave him the best possible care. And it wasn't that I couldn't wait to leave work. I enjoy what I do and most days have to peel myself away. It's just that there was something *so* exciting about seeing him again.

Most times when I drove in the driveway, I'd see his little head peeking out the window right beside the door. As I walked towards the house, I'd smile and wave. You could tell that Lucas was just exploding inside. He could hardly contain himself. And, as I got closer and closer, I found my own level of anticipation and excitement rising. I couldn't wait to get there.

When I got to the door, this is what would happen: I'd knock on the little window where Lucas had practically glued his face. Then Darlene or I would open the door a crack. Before I could even step inside, Lucas would shoot towards me, jump up, and wrap his arms around my neck. What a feeling! Nothing that happened during the course of a day could compare with this all out, emotionally charged, it's-so-good-to-see-you greeting.

Jesus tells a story that depicts this same kind of greeting. A young man goes away for a period of time. He makes some bad choices, things don't work out too well for him, and he decides to return home, even though he's a little afraid of the reception he might get from his father. According to the story, "When he was still a long way off, his father saw him. His heart pounding, [the father] ran out, embraced him, and kissed him."

That's how *I* felt when I saw Lucas at the end of the day. My heart pounded. It literally started to beat faster. My pace quickened because I couldn't wait to see him. We'd embrace and hug and kiss, each so happy to see the other.

- How do you greet the people near and dear to you? Do you show excitement when you see your spouse at the end of the day, when your kids come home from school? Do you embrace the people you care about with your words and your actions?
- Are you aware that God greets you, no matter where you've been or what you've done, with the same kind of unconditional love the father showed the son? Do you realize that God's heart beats faster as God moves to embrace us with arms wide open?

A word with God

O God, who greets me day after day, thank you for your unconditional love that continues to grace me. Help me to express my joy for those that I meet today, and to feel that excitement of meeting again. Thank you for the people in my life who inspire me to say, "How good it is to see you," each time we are together. As I share my own love with others, may they experience your love for them. In the name of Jesus I pray. Amen.

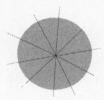

A Little Boost

You yourselves have seen what I did to Egypt,
and how I carried you on eagles' wings and brought you to myself.
EXODUS 19:4

Often when I went to pick up Lucas from his caregiver Darlene, I would find him outside playing with Darlene's son Christopher. Though Christopher was several years older than Lucas, they were good buddies. Lucas was like Christopher's shadow and *had* to do, or at least *try* to do, whatever Christopher did.

One day I found them playing basketball in the driveway. The hoop was slightly lower than regulation, so it was no problem for Christopher. However, Lucas wasn't even two yet, so for him it was a *long* way up. He would stand under the hoop and, with both hands, throw the ball as high as he could. And still it would only make it halfway.

After a few tries, Lucas understandably got a bit frustrated. I couldn't bear to watch anymore, so I picked him up and held him as high as I could over my shoulders. It was just the boost he needed. Now he was able to put the ball right in.

Talk about excitement. He was just like the big boys now. From then on, every time we were around a basketball net, Lucas would run to me with arms up and say "Daddy shoot?!"

Helping Lucas play basketball brought me great joy. I loved seeing him reach his goal. It also pleased me to enable Lucas to do something that on his own he wouldn't have been able to do. We made a good team and we both benefited!

Sometimes we encounter things in life that are too much for us to handle on our own. We need a boost. Often, that boost is all we need to reach what had seemed like an unreachable goal, or to overcome an obstacle we thought we could never overcome. All we need is a little encouragement, some extra strength, a bit of assurance or hope, and the ability to relax and, for a moment, find the peace that allows us to put our anxieties aside.

These are boosts that God can offer us. And the great thing is that God is just as pleased to give us these boosts as we are to receive them.

- As you think about God's desire and ability to offer you a boost, consider the areas of your life where this might be of benefit. And, as you do this, let these words from Exodus sift through your mind and heart: "I carried you on eagles' wings and brought you to myself..."

A word with God

Dear God, I am challenged by some areas of my life. Left on my own, I become frustrated and overwhelmed. Thanks for your promise to walk with me and raise me up. Together, I trust that we can rise above any obstacles I may face. Let's fly together today. In Christ's name I pray. Amen.

Just Throwing Stones

You also, like living stones, are being built into a spiritual house…
1 PETER 2:4

Throwing stones was one of Lucas' favorite things to do. But it was at Lake Louise, in Alberta, Canada, that I realized just *how much* he loved to do it. If you've ever been there, you'll remember the view; it is one of the most spectacular in the world – a gorgeous turquoise-colored lake surrounded by glacier-capped mountains. Confronted with this incredible sight, do you know what Lucas found the most pleasure in? Throwing stones!

Lucas would throw stones anywhere. It didn't need to be Lake Louise. It didn't have to be a cliff with a spectacular view and a 50-foot drop. He'd throw stones into a field. He'd throw stones onto the road (not something we encouraged!). He'd throw stones anywhere.

And it didn't have to be a certain kind of stone. It didn't have to be a certain size or a certain color or a particular shape or texture. There's a creek behind our house that has this little bridge crossing over it. Lucas could not cross that bridge without throwing a stone into the water. Often we could only find tiny pebbles. It didn't matter. Lucas could make use of any stone. Sometimes, he'd even throw with both hands. *Always*, he'd have a huge smile on his face, as if this were the first time he'd ever done it.

God loves to throw stones, too. And do you know who the stones are? We are. As 1 Peter 2:4 says, "You also, like living stones, are being built into a spiritual house…" We are the living stones that God "throws" out into the world.

Just as throwing stones put a smile on Lucas' face, I like to think that God smiles every time one of us recognizes that we are a stone which God desires to build upon. And just as Lucas could use any and every stone, so God can use each of us – our size or age or looks just don't matter. God looks at each of us, as different as we are, with loving adoration. And finally, just as Lucas would throw stones in any location with the same level of energy and hope, so God can use us, no matter where we are. It makes no difference whether we're teachers, or doctors, or home-care workers, or computer consultants, or flipping burgers, or running our own business. We all have the opportunity and the responsibility to make an impact on the people in our life. It's all part of being one of God's stones.

• **How are you going to be a living stone today? Where are you going to go? Who are you going to be with? And, can you see God smiling as you go?**

A word with God

Today I pray that I might be a living stone, someone who impacts others in a way that shows my love for you, dear God. Help me to know the importance of my role, and that even the smallest smile, greeting, or helping hand can make a difference in someone else's life. May your church build upon me! Amen.

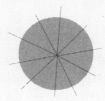

Love at Every Sight!

But we were gentle among you, like a nurse tenderly caring for her own children.
So deeply do we care for you that we are determined to share with you
not only the gospel of God, but also our own selves,
because you have become very dear to us.

1 THESSALONIANS 2:7B–8

Many say that the only thing better than becoming a parent is becoming a grandparent. This was definitely true for my parents, especially for my dad.

My dad was not the type to readily show affection, partly due, no doubt, to his own makeup, and partly due to the way love was expressed in his home when he was growing up. But becoming a grandparent changed all that.

I never could have imagined my dad waiting at the door for us to arrive. But he did when his grandson Lucas was coming! Or my dad encouraging my mom to buy something. But he did when it was for his grandson Lucas! Or my dad changing a diaper? Well, maybe he didn't do that, but I bet he would have if he'd had to!

The point is, my dad had a very special relationship with Lucas. Often, when my folks came to see us, here's what would happen.

Lucas would see my dad and run towards him. Dad would pick him up and Lucas would affectionately cry, "Paaapaaa!" My dad would just as affectionately cry, "Luuucaaaas!" They'd go back and forth: "Paaaapaaa!" "Luuucaaas!" "Paaapaaa!" "Luuucaaas!"

I'm not sure who was more proud and content. It was so obvious that grandfather and grandson had developed a bond that not everyone gets the opportunity to experience.

This was the type of relationship that Paul appears to have had with the Thessalonians. He uses phrases such as "so deeply do we care for you" and "you have become very dear to us." Seems like there was a special bond there, too.

- **Who are you very close to? Who do you care deeply about? Do they know? Do you show them and tell them every time you see them? Why not pick someone and do it today. Send them an e-mail telling them how much you appreciate them. Call them for no reason other than to tell them how deeply you care for them. If you can do that, you'll be a step closer to the type of relationships God intends for us.**

A word with God

Thank you for those special relationships in my life. It is such a blessing to be able to know love in this way. Help me to constantly foster these relationships and to never take them for granted. Thank you for your love for me, loving God. Amen.

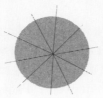

Make a Joyful Noise

Worship the Lord with gladness; come before him with joyful songs.
PSALM 100:2

It doesn't matter how old we are. Whether we're one or 100, music has the power to touch our soul, to inspire the deepest parts of our being, and to generally get our blood pumping.

Lucas loved music. In the car, he'd listen to tapes we put on. Often, he couldn't wait for the next song to come on when one had finished. He'd get so impatient with the "dead air" between songs he'd start yelling, "Again! Again! Again!"

Of course, most of us who enjoy music have some favorite songs. Lucas had a few. One of them was a song we sing in church called *I Love You, Lord*. The words are easy to remember and the tune is one that even a non-musical person such as myself can sing.

Because it was so simple, I started singing that song to Lucas from the time he was just a baby. When I walked him around our little apartment in the middle of the night, this was the song that I would sing to try to comfort him. The great thing was that sometimes it even worked. And when it didn't help him, at least it helped me.

As Lucas got older, his love for music grew. This meant that, among other things, he learned who could sing and who couldn't. One night when I was changing him, I started to sing "I love you, Lord, and I lift my voice…" Lucas stopped me and said, "No, Daddy! Mommy sing!" He knew enough to know that his mom could sing in tune and his dad couldn't!

But the truth is, it didn't really matter too much whether the music was in tune or not. Whether it was in the car, at church, before bedtime, first thing in the morning, out for a walk, whatever, it didn't matter. Music always brought Lucas joy. It lifted his spirits and put a smile on his face.

Music can soothe. It can heal. It can express things that sometimes mere words can't express. Music offers feelings as well as insights. It can connect with the elderly as well as with infants in the womb. Music is powerful and wonderful and one of God's greatest gifts.

Psalm 100 says, "Shout for joy to the Lord, all the earth…come before God with joyful songs. Know that the Lord is God." It can be through something as simple as music that we realize again that God is real. As our toe begins to tap and our heart beats faster and the music moves through us we can feel life and faith and our Creator in new and refreshing ways.

- What is your favorite kind of music?
- If you wanted to try to experience the presence of God through music, what music would you choose?
- Are you open to experiencing God in the music you hear today?

A word with God

O God, thank you for the gift of music. Today, let music put me in touch with you and allow me to carry you with me wherever I go. Amen.

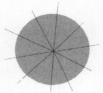

Running the Bases

I do not consider that I have made it my own; but this one thing I do:
forgetting what lies behind and straining forward to what lies ahead,
I press on toward the goal for the prize of the heavenly call of God in Christ Jesus.
PHILIPPIANS 3:13

It was an exciting day. Lucas' friend Matthew was turning 2, and Lucas had been invited to the birthday party. Unfortunately, I wasn't able to attend but I heard all about it. There had been a grab bag with lots of good candies and prizes. There had been cake and ice cream. They had played a number of different games and he had made some new friends.

But for Lucas, it was the baseball game in the backyard that was the most memorable. One of the gifts had been a T-ball set, which was immediately put into action. The older kids had played this before, but for the two-year-olds, this was completely *new*! What a cool thing to do – hit the ball, then run like crazy! Lucas loved it. And he remembered this little sequence for days and weeks after the party. He repeated it with passion. He repeated it with life. He repeated it as if he were playing in front of thousands and thousands of fans.

At various times, out of the blue, Lucas would do a pretend swing of the bat and as he did it he'd say, "Hit!" Then he'd take off somewhere – perhaps down the hallway or over to the couch, or in a circle around our yard. As he did *that*, he'd say, "Run!" He was reenacting the experience of running the bases. First you hit the ball, and then you run.

It was the look of determination on Lucas' face as he did this that I found most amazing. He put everything he had into it. He had a goal to accomplish and you'd better not get in his way. He had to run around the bases. And it was so much fun that he had to do it over and over again. "Hit" and "run." "Hit" and "run." "Hit" and "run."

Lucas' attitude of strength and determination reminded me of Paul's words to the Philippians: "I do not consider that I have made it my own; but this one thing I do: forgetting what lies behind and straining forward to what lies ahead, I press on toward the goal for the prize of the heavenly call of God in Christ Jesus."

Paul was encouraging the Philippians to press on. He was saying, in his own way, "Don't worry about your last at bat. Just get up to the plate and make this a good one. Keep running the bases. Keep swinging. Keep running. Keep working. Keep reaching and striving. Keep pressing on."

- **What are you passionate about? What makes your heart beat faster and puts a fire in your belly?**
- **What goal do you think is worth pressing towards? When you peel away the layers, details, and obligations in your life, what do you most want to strive towards?**

A word with God

Dear God, life can be such a race sometimes, and we can even feel like we're running in circles. Forgive me for the times I have remained stuck in the failures of the past, unable to look ahead. Help me to clarify my goals and destinations this week, and most of all, to run towards you, Christ Jesus. Amen.

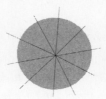

Whose Church Is It?

Now you are the body of Christ, and individually members of it.
1 CORINTHIANS 12:27

It's amazing how observant children are, from a very young age. We were reminded of this as we drove to church one Sunday morning and Lucas asked, "We going to Daddy's church?" Lucas had recognized where we were going and he also knew that this was where Daddy worked, so he figured it made sense to call it "Daddy's church."

Well, I knew I didn't own the church and so it didn't seem right for Lucas to call it "Daddy's church." I quickly responded, "Lucas, it's not Daddy's church; it's *your* church." I wanted to make sure he knew that even as a two-year-old it was just as much his church as mine. I wanted church to be a place where he felt belonging and meaning and acceptance and love.

I think Lucas liked the idea. He thought for a moment and then repeated what I'd said. "My church?" Lucas asked.

"Yes, Lucas, *your* church," I replied.

Of course the truth is that none of us "owns" the church. It is *Christ's* church and we partner with him. That's what Peter discovered in his conversation with Jesus. Jesus said to Peter, "And I tell you that you are Peter, and on this rock I will build my church" (Matthew 16:18).

It's *our* church, not just in the sense that we find a place where we belong and are accepted. That's certainly part of it. But it's also *our* church because we play a role. Christ's church will only prevail if we, like Peter, become the rock upon which it is built. Christ invites us to be part of something bigger than ourselves. We can participate in the healing of our land. We can make a difference in the lives of real people. We can spread good news, feed the hungry, visit the lonely.

You can see why I wanted to make sure that Lucas knew it wasn't just "Daddy's church." It's not just me. The "rock" that Christ's church is built upon is much bigger than the minister or the chair of the board or the church secretary or the Sunday school superintendent or the matriarch who has been at the church since it started. We all must bring our different gifts to the table and join in.

The church as Jesus intended is a place where all people can belong. It's a community where people care for one another and for the world around them. It's a place where each person gives of themselves in order to carry out Christ's mission.

- **Are you at a point where you can say "my" church? Do you feel like part of the "rock" on which Christ is building his church?**

A word with God

Thank you, God, for this community called the church. Help me to claim it as my own, and to offer my gifts and energies to make up the body of Christ. Build upon me, I pray. Amen.

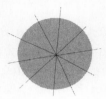

Still Love Me?

I have loved you with an everlasting love,
therefore I have continued my faithfulness to you.
JEREMIAH 31:3

Learning the rules of life is all part of growing up. But some days this process can create some really difficult moments. At least it did the day Katrina was teaching Lucas the rules for walking to the park.

Sure we encouraged Lucas to walk with us and to hold our hand. But he liked to do it himself and to run ahead a little bit. That was fine. There was really only one rule that could not be broken: *Whatever you do, don't go on the road!*

We lived in a townhouse complex at the time and there were always lots of cars driving through. To make matters worse, the sidewalk that led to the park crossed the road at a corner – a *dangerous* corner, where cars might not see a little boy until it was too late. Hence the "whatever you do, don't go on the road" rule!

You can probably anticipate where this is going. Katrina was taking Lucas to the park (or maybe it was Lucas who was taking Katrina). Either way, the road rule got broken. Lucas ran ahead. As he approached the road, Katrina called after him reminding him to stop. But he just kept on going. Katrina was both scared and furious. The fun trip to the park was over before it had even begun. Katrina picked Lucas up and carried him home like a football tucked under her arm, except that footballs don't usually make so much noise. This little red-haired football cried and whined all the way home: "Want to go to the park! Don't want to go home!"

The decision had been made. It was too late. And now no one was happy. Lucas sat on the stairs in our front hallway and cried. He was so upset.

I wonder if any of the following thoughts ran through his little head and heart:

How could I have been so dumb? I knew I shouldn't have done it. I just didn't stop to think. Mom must really be frustrated with me. She's so good to me and then I go and blow it. She must really be upset to bring me right home. Next time I'll listen. Next time I'll do it right. I hope there is a next time. I hope Mom still loves me. Or have I blown that too?

We all have messy battles with our children at times. We may get angry and frustrated. We may need to get out of the house for some space. But we never stop loving our children. It's just like God says to the people of Jeremiah's time: "I have loved you with an everlasting love, therefore I have continued my faithfulness to you."

God loves us with an everlasting love. It's a love that will not let go. It's a love that is real. It's a love that remains, regardless of our circumstances or how we feel about ourselves. It's a love that we don't need to earn. It's a love that is unconditional. It's a love that lasts forever.

- Have you done things that you regret?
- Do you feel that God just might not forgive you for "this one"?
- Can you open yourself to the reality that God loves you – even if you're not able to love yourself?

A word with God

Gracious God, it is so hard to comprehend your love for me sometimes – it is just so deep, this love that continues to be there no matter what I do, or how far I might stray from your presence. Thank you for your everlasting love, your unconditional love, your love expressed so beautifully in the person of Jesus Christ, in whose name I pray. Amen.

The Grocery Store Bun

*I am the bread of life. Whoever comes to me will never be hungry,
and whoever believes in me will never be thirsty.*

JOHN 6:35

It was one of those everyday activities that became special. Every Monday morning, Lucas and I would drop Katrina off at the school where she taught. Then we'd head over to our local grocery store to buy our weekly groceries. By the time we got down the first aisle, Lucas would have his face full of fresh bun.

You see, I found that if I gave Lucas a bun it kept him happy. If he *didn't* get the bun, he would want to get down from the cart and run around. If that happened, I knew we'd never get done. Fortunately, the bakery area was located at the end of the first aisle.

This also meant that I needed to have the items on our list in the grocery cart by the time he finished eating. As he came closer to finishing, I would go faster and faster through the store. There were days when I wished the bun would not disappear and that Lucas could keep eating.

Wouldn't it be great if there was a type of bun that you could just keep eating and eating? Or maybe a loaf of bread that never ran out of slices? Imagine being fed with something that prevented you from getting hungry a couple hours later?

What if, instead of food, we were talking about the spiritual hunger that many people experience? Could there be something we might eat that would satisfy our longing for peace? Is it possible that something might exist, that could connect with our yearning for hope in this world and in our lives?

Jesus said to some people one day, "I am the bread of life. Whoever comes to me will never be hungry and whoever believes in me will never be thirsty." Jesus offers humanity a slice of life that feeds the innermost parts of our being. Jesus reveals a type of love that nourishes us in ways that nothing else can.

- **Have you been searching for something beyond yourself? What sorts of things feed your soul? Could today be the day to let God take care of your hunger pains? The table is prepared. All is ready for you. Come take a seat.**

A word with God

Dear God, I have known that spiritual hunger deep in my soul, and I know that only you can fulfill any emptiness that I feel. I open myself to you today. Fill me with your bread of life, your love, your compassion, that I may feel whole and complete. Thank you for this great, everlasting gift. In Jesus' name I pray. Amen.

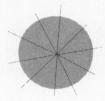

The Key to Getting There

God will wipe every tear from their eyes.
Death will be no more; mourning and crying and pain will be no more,
for the first things have passed away.
REVELATION 21:4

Lucas, like most children, went through a period of time when he would wake up very early. On one of these mornings, I decided to take him to the park so that Katrina could sleep in a bit. I figured there was no sense in all of us being up so early.

So Lucas and I went to the park just down the road from us. Lucas always loved to go there because of its slides and things to climb on and because of the cool bridge that crossed over the stream.

After spending some time in the park, I realized it was time to go home. Though it was a weekend, we had someplace we needed to be by a certain time and in order for that to happen I knew we needed to get back and get things rolling.

I also knew that there was no way Lucas would want to leave. Because it was breakfast time and I knew that Lucas loved pancakes and that we had been planning on having a special pancake breakfast, I said, "Lucas, do you want to go home and have some pancakes?"

"Yes, please!" he replied, and we were on our way.

But then we came to a really big puddle. Lucas could not help himself. There was no way he could just walk by. So he stopped to wade. I said, "Lucas, remember we're going to go home and have pancakes!" He looked at me, acknowledged our common goal, and we were on our way once more.

Then he saw the tennis ball in the gutter. A tennis ball! A tennis ball! *This* looks like fun. Once again he got distracted. So I said again, "Lucas, remember we're going home to have pancakes." The 'Oh Ya!' light shone on his face, and we continued on towards our destination.

Until we passed someone walking with their beautiful dog. Lucas loved dogs. He could not pass a dog without stopping to pet it. I wondered how I would get him home now. So I said, "Lucas, remember we're going home to have some pancakes." Lucas gave the dog one last pet and we were on our way.

The key to getting Lucas home was to continuously point out what lay ahead. It was worth leaving the park and the puddle and the ball and the dog because we were going to have pancakes. With that vision of a preferred future before us, we were able to keep going despite all the distractions.

John, the writer of the Book of Revelation, offers us a vision, a picture of a preferred future that makes the distractions of our lives worth leaving behind as we move ahead. Those distractions are not always pleasurable. They include sadness, pain, depression, disappointment. But the vision of

God's future that John offers us is of a world in which there *are* no more tears, no more pain, and no more sorrow, a world where everything will be as it should be. Let that be the vision to keep us going, let it be the key to getting through any distraction.

- **What distractions are you dealing with today?**
- **What can you do to help sharpen the vision of God's future?**
- **Will it keep you going?**

A word with God

This world sometimes brings so many distractions that deter us from the joy you intend for us, dear God. Today I want to clearly see your world as you want it to be. Fill me with your joy and your vision. Help me to share it with others, that we all might continue on this journey of faith strengthened and renewed.

The Stairs Story

When Jesus saw her weeping and the Jews who came with her also weeping,
he was greatly disturbed in spirit and deeply moved…Jesus began to weep.

JOHN 11:33–35

Every parent has a "stairs story." It's one of those shared experiences we've all had, when one of our children has the misfortune of falling down the stairs. By the time it happens, it's too late and there's nothing you can do about it…

One day I was with Lucas on our front steps. He was at the stage where he was able to walk, but stairs were hit and miss. It was necessary to stay close to him, especially on the front steps, because they were made of concrete.

I stayed right behind him, until we got to the top. I thought he had made it, so I turned to get something out of the mailbox. The second I turned my back, he went tumbling down the stairs. My heart sank. I dropped whatever was in my hand and leapt down the stairs towards him. I picked him up and I wrapped my arms around him. "It's going to okay, Lucas," I said, "It's going to be okay."

Sometimes people wonder and question where God is when bad things happen. When someone dies in a car accident. When an earthquake kills thousands. When a snowmobile goes through the ice. When a tumor or an aneurysm takes a life. When a youth strikes their head on the bottom of a pool and is left in a wheelchair. When tragedy strikes, where is God? When horror hits, what is God's response?

I believe God's heart sinks just like mine did when Lucas fell down those concrete stairs. God leaps towards us; God wants to pick us up and embrace us with ever-loving arms. God says to us, "My precious, precious child. Hang in there, it's going to be okay."

Jesus was faced with a tragedy in his day. A man named Lazarus, whom Jesus knew and loved, became ill and died. Do you know what Jesus' response was? When Jesus saw the family weeping, he "was greatly disturbed in spirit and deeply moved" and "Jesus began to weep." In and through Jesus we discover God's response to us.

When pain and heartache and despair hit, we are not left all alone. God cries with us. This doesn't take away the hurt, but it can enable us to live and survive and even thrive, despite our loss.

Whatever challenges you face today, know that we have a God who doesn't desire for bad things to happen. Rather, we have a God who seeks to enter into our lives and to meet us where we are.

- **Have you "fallen down the stairs" in your life?**
- **In what areas of hurt do you need to feel God's presence?**

- Are you able to let yourself be embraced by the God of the universe?
- Where might you "hear" God saying everything is going to be okay?

A word with God

O God, sometimes the pain of this world is too much to bear on my own. Thank you for weeping with me. Thank you for your encouragement and care that comes through those people who surround me. I pray for Christ's healing today for myself and those I love. Amen.

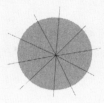

Where's Howie?

Ask, and it will be given you; search, and you will find;
knock, and the door will be opened for you.
For everyone who asks receives and everyone who searches finds,
and for everyone who knocks, the door will be opened.
MATTHEW 7:7-8

Have you ever had to try to keep a small child quiet early in the morning when others are sleeping? I discovered the difficulty of that while visiting my brother in Alberta. Because of the time change, Lucas was waking up before 6:00 a.m.

I would try to get him to whisper, but it didn't work. I'd say, "Lucas, we need to be quiet so everyone can sleep." And he'd yell out, "Why?" as he dragged his high chair across the hardwood floor, making noises that would stir the deepest of sleepers.

One morning we were eating breakfast in the dining room. Lucas was in his high chair and he kept saying something to me that I couldn't quite understand. Each time he repeated it and I didn't get it, he'd say it again, even louder. Finally, after getting to the point where he was practically yelling and there was no hope of anyone sleeping anymore, I heard a voice from above. It wasn't God (though some might say it was pretty close!). It was Katrina calling down from our bedroom to shed some light on this mystery phrase. "He's asking for Howie," she informed me.

Howie was a little stuffed owl. Lucas could see Howie from his high chair and he *really* wanted to let me know. Howie, you see, had become one of the biggest hits of our holidays. Hiding Howie and then trying to find him again had become a very exciting game which Lucas played with our young friend Emily Allin. They would play this game for hours on end – in the car, in the backyard, while watching TV… And each time, Lucas' eyes would sparkle as he and Emily discovered the thrill of finding Howie all over again.

Ever get a sparkle in your eye when you find something that means a lot to you? Love? A new hobby? The home you and your spouse have always wanted? A good friend? A family member you haven't seen for a long time? That special gift you'd been looking for? The shirt you'd lost and thought was gone? The job you've always dreamed of?

Jesus says, "Ask, and it will be given you; search, and you will find; knock, and the door will be opened for you. For everyone who asks receives and everyone who searches finds, and for everyone who knocks, the door will be opened."

"Where's Howie" isn't just a game for kids. It's part of life. Just change "Howie" to whatever it is that you are currently looking for. This includes some of the deeper things most of us look for at various times in our life.

Peace in our beings? Guidance for our lives? Encouragement to keep us going? Love to know we're cared for and not alone?

- **What kinds of things have you been looking for lately?**
- **How might you turn to God for help in your search?**

A word with God

Gracious God, thank you for encouraging us to ask for the things we long for, and to seek until we find. May I experience the excitement of finding that which is so precious to me this week, whether in a simple moment or in a big decision. I am thankful that I have found you and your love in my life, which alone can bring a sparkle to my eye. Amen.

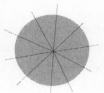

Sweet Memories

Jesus said, "Let the little children come to me, and do not stop them;
for it is to such as these that the kingdom of heaven belongs."
MATTHEW 19:14

One of the neat things about being part of a church community is the way your family seems to expand. Your children suddenly have three or four grandmothers, countless aunts and uncles, and a whole bunch of cousins! Usually, there are one, perhaps two, that are tops on the list. For us, that one was Connie.

Connie had always been like a surrogate grandmother to Lucas. She didn't just spend time with him in the nursery at church. She had Lucas to her condominium and cared for him on numerous occasions. She bought him little gifts every once in a while. Her eyes sparkled whenever she saw him. She didn't look after Lucas just to help us out. She did it because she really, genuinely, loved and adored him.

Which is partly why this particular moment continues to bring a smile to her face. It always will.

We had planned for Lucas to spend a few hours at Connie's home one afternoon while we went out with some friends. It had been a few weeks since Lucas had seen Connie, so we weren't exactly sure how he would respond. We needn't have worried.

As soon as we got off the elevator we could see Connie standing outside her doorway, about 20 meters away at the end of the hallway. When Lucas saw Connie, he took off running towards her. I couldn't see his face, of course, only his little red head bouncing down the hall, his arms spread wide. I could, however, see Connie's face. That's what *I'll* remember.

Connie was beaming with pride. Her face shone with life. This was truly a match made in heaven and this moment was putting an exclamation mark on that fact. The open love and appreciation for one another that was revealed in this hallway greeting went deep into the hearts of both Connie and Lucas. *This* was a moment of truth. *This* was the way life was meant to be lived and the way love was meant to be expressed.

So often we discover the simple yet profound truths of life through the innocent, authentic, and vulnerable ways of a child. That is, in many ways, what this very book has been about. God speaks to us, reaches out to us, in a variety of ways. One of those is most certainly through the eyes and ears and the hands and mouths of children.

On one of Jesus' busier days, some people brought their children to see him. The disciples brushed them off. Maybe they thought Jesus was stooping too low. Maybe they thought he didn't have the time. I'm not sure why the disciples did it. But we do know Jesus' response.

Jesus said, "Let the little children come to me, and do not stop them; for it is to such as these that the kingdom of heaven belongs."

We can experience little tastes of heaven through the lives of our children.
- **Have you had one of those moments lately? If you don't have a child of your own, have you seen glimpses of the God-life in other people's children, and can you find a way to share in it?**

We hope that you have enjoyed sharing some of the sweet memories that are engraved on our hearts, and that the lessons we learned in our two short years with Lucas will be a gift that you, too, can cherish.

A word with God

What a gift you have given us in the form of children. From their smiles to their words to their actions, their innocence and openness can give us glimpses of your great love. Let us never take for granted the value of spending time with children, remembering that it is to these that the kingdom of heaven belongs. What a grand place it must be! Amen.